THE JOB COACH FOR YOUNG PROFESSIONALS

The Workbook for Landing the Right Job

By Susan Kennedy
and
Karen Baker

CAREER *treking* ⟹

Putting Careers in Motion

Intern Bridge

The Job Coach for Young Professionals: The Workbook for Landing the Right Job

By Susan Kennedy and Karen Baker

This publication is designed to provide accurate and authoritative information in regard to the subject matter covered. It is sold with the understanding that neither the author nor the publisher is engaged in rendering legal, accounting, or other professional service. If legal advice or other expert assistance is required, the services of a competent professional should be sought.

Further, although every precaution has been taken in the preparation of this book, the authors and publisher assume no responsibility for errors or omissions. Nor is any liability assumed for damages resulting from the use of the information contained herein.

Published by Intern Bridge, Inc.
19 Railroad Street, Suite 3B
Acton, MA 01720

For sales information, please email Sales@InternBridge.com or call us at 800-531-6091.

Cover design/layout/production: web.me.com/bookpackgraphics/Bookpack_Graphics (Dan Berger)

Printed in U.S.A.

YOUR JOB SEARCH

You are reading this because you are most likely about to graduate from college, just graduated, or have even spent a year or two working at a job in which you are not happy. Many students look at their college years as the time in their life when they are preparing themselves for their future career. What is typically missing in their college education is learning about the job search process. Your college degree is only one piece of information that an employer uses when they are deciding whether to hire you or not. How you present yourself, how you articulate who you are and what you are capable of, is just as important as the degree you have just earned.

The Job Coach for Young Professionals provides you with exercises which will help identify the right job, prepare to interview for that job, sell yourself to prospective employers, and finally, succeed in your desired career. The initial idea for this book came from observations of thousands of entry level candidates we have interviewed. We found they were frequently unprepared for their interviews and lacked the ability to articulate who they are and why they are the best person for the job. That need led to the development of our job coaching business. As the business grew, there was a demand for us to document our process. These strategies have been used for years in our coaching sessions and have now been adapted for use as an essential guide for every young professional to use on their own. This workbook can be used throughout your career – after all, knowing how to look for a job is a life skill.

The Job Coach for Young Professionals offers four steps to success.

Assess Myself
In this section, you will determine what you are good at, what you like to do, and what types of jobs and companies interest you. In order to identify these jobs and companies, you will:

- Complete a variety of Skills, Interests and Values Assessments.
- Identify and research job possibilities which are right for you.
- Determine gaps in your experience which may become obstacles to securing the right job.

By the end of this section you will have set short and long-term career goals which identify potential "best fit" jobs, industries and companies. Clear and specific career goals are the driver of a successful job search.

Prepare Myself

The second section of this process will help you clearly articulate how your past experience has prepared you for the jobs you are going after. In this section you will:

- Answer the question "Tell me about yourself." This is one of the hardest interview questions to answer. The successful answer will help you stand out in a very competitive playing field.
- Learn how to demonstrate your skills and abilities during an interview.
- Develop a compelling resume.
- Prepare insightful questions for the interviewer.
- Present yourself professionally during interviews.

When you have completed this section, you will not walk out of another job interview feeling unprepared.

Sell Myself

The third step helps you to plan and implement a successful job search. How many resumes have you posted to job boards? Given that there is a 4% success rate and a thousand other people have responded to those job boards, you probably received no response. You need to set yourself apart from the competition. The most successful tactic to finding a job is networking. In this section you will:

- Develop a Job Search Action Plan.
- Learn strategies for how and with whom to network.
- Use tools to help you stay organized

Succeed

Most people think that finding the right job is the hard part – and it is. However, keeping it can be just as challenging. The fourth and final section of this workbook will help you make the transition from school to work. This section provides you with

- Keys To Success in the workplace.
- Tools to prepare for your new job.

TABLE OF CONTENTS

The first step in any successful job search is knowing what you want to do and why. To begin this process, it's important to think about how you want your life to look 4 or 5 years from now. Do you want to live in a city or a suburb? What type of work environment motivates you? Do you prefer to work on your own or as part of a team? Is graduate school a possibility?

For Example:

Where do you want to live?
I'd like to be living on my own (not in my parents' house), preferably in a city. I like NYC but realize it's expensive; maybe Boston.

Work environment?
I want to be heard and be able to express my ideas. I'd like a more casual environment.

Growth in career?
Possibly go for my master's degree in the evenings. I'd like for there to be training opportunities as well as maybe work with a mentor at my company.

Outside interests?

I'd like to keep doing my fundraising for the American Cancer Society.

Other Thoughts...

I'm not sure how or where, but I want to know I'm on the right path in 2-3 years.

Take a few minutes to write down some notes. Revisit this page throughout the process. You may want to add to your vision or change it depending on the jobs you choose to pursue.

Where do you want to live? (suburb or city; what city or part of the country)

_____

_____

_____

_____

ENVISIONING YOUR FUTURE

Work environment (large or small company; casual or professional; work at home; travel)

_____

_____

_____

_____

_____

_____

Growth in career (run the company some day; work/life balance; training; additional schooling; master's degree)

_____

_____

_____

_____

_____

_____

Outside interests (volunteer work/community service; hobbies; sports; family; travel)

_____

_____

_____

_____

_____

_____

Other thoughts...

_____

_____

_____

The next step is actually assessing who you are and researching what you want to do. You will evaluate your background, your achievements, what you're good at (and what you're not so good at), as well as what's important to you in the workplace. Knowing who you are and what motivates you will be the foundation of your job search. Once you have identified your skills, interests, and values, you will begin the research stage. That is, you will be looking at specific job titles and industries, as well as potential employers.

Each step in this job search process is designed to build upon itself. Each step was created to help you translate You into the world of work. Complete each step in order, but it doesn't have to be done all at once. This process will take a lot of thinking. Take the time you need to complete it as accurately as you can.

The Assessment Process is depicted in the chart below:

ASSESS MYSELF PROCESS

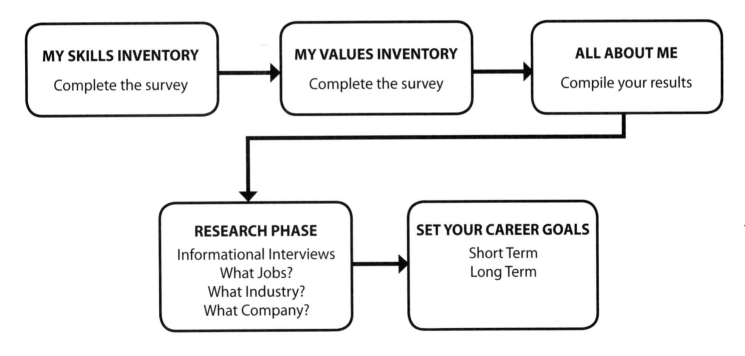

— Complete My Skills Inventory and My Values Inventory. As you complete these exercises, you may want to talk to some friends and family members to verify your thoughts (or to jog your memory!).

MY SKILLS INVENTORY

Think back to your work experiences, internships and school experiences.

Rate the following skills based on your mastery and comfort level with each one by circling the appropriate number.

> A score of 7 = strong skill
>
> A score of 1 = low skill, no experience or not comfortable with this skill

In the right hand column, rate your interest in using each skill in your career.

> A score of 7 = a very strong interest in using the skill in your career
>
> A score of 1= no interest

Add up your score at the end of each section.

Written Communication Skills	**Skill Level**	**Interest Level**
1. Experience writing technical or logical reports	1 2 3 4 5 6 7	1 2 3 4 5 6 7
2. Creative writing skills, i.e., poetry, fiction, plays	1 2 3 4 5 6 7	1 2 3 4 5 6 7
3. Draft proposals, i.e., for group projects	1 2 3 4 5 6 7	1 2 3 4 5 6 7
4. Experience writing copy for sales/advertising pieces	1 2 3 4 5 6 7	1 2 3 4 5 6 7
5. Edit and proofread written documents	1 2 3 4 5 6 7	1 2 3 4 5 6 7
6. Use all forms of technology for writing	1 2 3 4 5 6 7	1 2 3 4 5 6 7
7. Strong knowledge and use of appropriate writing format, i.e., business letters or case studies	1 2 3 4 5 6 7	1 2 3 4 5 6 7
TOTAL:	_____	_____

Analytical Skills	**Skill Level**	**Interest Level**
1. Research and analyze data and arrive at a solution	1 2 3 4 5 6 7	1 2 3 4 5 6 7
2. Analyze quantitative, physical and/or scientific data	1 2 3 4 5 6 7	1 2 3 4 5 6 7
3. Document analysis of study, research and results	1 2 3 4 5 6 7	1 2 3 4 5 6 7
4. Assess/compare information to research & investigate	1 2 3 4 5 6 7	1 2 3 4 5 6 7
5. Apply curiosity	1 2 3 4 5 6 7	1 2 3 4 5 6 7
6. Create insightful and pertinent questions	1 2 3 4 5 6 7	1 2 3 4 5 6 7
7. Comfortable using technology for statistical analysis	1 2 3 4 5 6 7	1 2 3 4 5 6 7
TOTAL:	_____	_____

Organizational Skills

	Skill Level	Interest Level
1. Organize tasks to be done and develop a plan	1 2 3 4 5 6 7	1 2 3 4 5 6 7
2. Organize people, information and activities	1 2 3 4 5 6 7	1 2 3 4 5 6 7
3. Meet time schedules and deadlines	1 2 3 4 5 6 7	1 2 3 4 5 6 7
4. Foresee problems and provide solutions	1 2 3 4 5 6 7	1 2 3 4 5 6 7
5. Establish realistic goals and plans to achieve them	1 2 3 4 5 6 7	1 2 3 4 5 6 7
6. Create efficient processes	1 2 3 4 5 6 7	1 2 3 4 5 6 7
7. Ability to follow up to make sure the job is done	1 2 3 4 5 6 7	1 2 3 4 5 6 7

TOTAL: _____   _____

Verbal Communication Skills

	Skill Level	Interest Level
1. Public speaking in front of large groups of people	1 2 3 4 5 6 7	1 2 3 4 5 6 7
2. Influence others to a different point of view	1 2 3 4 5 6 7	1 2 3 4 5 6 7
3. Experience performing and entertaining	1 2 3 4 5 6 7	1 2 3 4 5 6 7
4. Express ideas to others who do not share your opinion	1 2 3 4 5 6 7	1 2 3 4 5 6 7
5. Experience selling products or services	1 2 3 4 5 6 7	1 2 3 4 5 6 7
6. Facilitate group or team discussions	1 2 3 4 5 6 7	1 2 3 4 5 6 7
7. Obtain information through interviewing /questioning people	1 2 3 4 5 6 7	1 2 3 4 5 6 7

TOTAL: _____   _____

Counseling and Serving Skills

	Skill Level	Interest Level
1. Provide consultation to help others	1 2 3 4 5 6 7	1 2 3 4 5 6 7
2. Show appropriate empathy and sensitivity to others	1 2 3 4 5 6 7	1 2 3 4 5 6 7
3. Encourage/guide people to make their own decisions	1 2 3 4 5 6 7	1 2 3 4 5 6 7
4. Listen with empathy and understanding	1 2 3 4 5 6 7	1 2 3 4 5 6 7
5. Inspire others to achieve goals	1 2 3 4 5 6 7	1 2 3 4 5 6 7
6. Help two parties keep the peace	1 2 3 4 5 6 7	1 2 3 4 5 6 7
7. Help others to see their capabilities	1 2 3 4 5 6 7	1 2 3 4 5 6 7

TOTAL: _____   _____

Interpersonal Skills

	Skill Level	Interest Level
1. Use humor when appropriate	1 2 3 4 5 6 7	1 2 3 4 5 6 7
2. Anticipate the needs of others	1 2 3 4 5 6 7	1 2 3 4 5 6 7
3. Communicate feelings appropriately	1 2 3 4 5 6 7	1 2 3 4 5 6 7
4. Understand human interactions; adapt to others	1 2 3 4 5 6 7	1 2 3 4 5 6 7
5. Resolve conflict between others	1 2 3 4 5 6 7	1 2 3 4 5 6 7
6. Communicate well with different groups of people	1 2 3 4 5 6 7	1 2 3 4 5 6 7
7. Build rapport easily and quickly	1 2 3 4 5 6 7	1 2 3 4 5 6 7

TOTAL: _____   _____

ASSESS MYSELF: My Skills and Interests Inventory

Research Skills	Skill Level	Interest Level
1. Pinpoint appropriate sources of information	1 2 3 4 5 6 7	1 2 3 4 5 6 7
2. Research all forms of information	1 2 3 4 5 6 7	1 2 3 4 5 6 7
3. Request information from appropriate sources	1 2 3 4 5 6 7	1 2 3 4 5 6 7
4. Make and verify assumptions; test for results	1 2 3 4 5 6 7	1 2 3 4 5 6 7
5. Classify and categorize information	1 2 3 4 5 6 7	1 2 3 4 5 6 7
6. Compile information from different sources	1 2 3 4 5 6 7	1 2 3 4 5 6 7
7. Search for hard to find data	1 2 3 4 5 6 7	1 2 3 4 5 6 7
TOTAL:	_____	_____

Nonverbal Communication Skills	Skill Level	Interest Level
1. Listen carefully and with interest	1 2 3 4 5 6 7	1 2 3 4 5 6 7
2. Make a good first impression	1 2 3 4 5 6 7	1 2 3 4 5 6 7
3. Use appropriate body language to express confidence	1 2 3 4 5 6 7	1 2 3 4 5 6 7
4. Convey a positive attitude	1 2 3 4 5 6 7	1 2 3 4 5 6 7
5. Make others feel comfortable through body language	1 2 3 4 5 6 7	1 2 3 4 5 6 7
6. Pick up on non-verbal cues	1 2 3 4 5 6 7	1 2 3 4 5 6 7
7. Demonstrate enthusiasm	1 2 3 4 5 6 7	1 2 3 4 5 6 7
TOTAL:	_____	_____

Training and Consulting Skills	Skill Level	Interest Level
1. Coach, teach, advise; ability to help others understand	1 2 3 4 5 6 7	1 2 3 4 5 6 7
2. Use all forms of media when creating a presentation	1 2 3 4 5 6 7	1 2 3 4 5 6 7
3. Create educational and informational materials	1 2 3 4 5 6 7	1 2 3 4 5 6 7
4. Run a group project or presentation	1 2 3 4 5 6 7	1 2 3 4 5 6 7
5. Explain and break down topics or ideas to others	1 2 3 4 5 6 7	1 2 3 4 5 6 7
6. Manage personality differences working in a group	1 2 3 4 5 6 7	1 2 3 4 5 6 7
7. Facilitate a team to agree on and recommend solutions	1 2 3 4 5 6 7	1 2 3 4 5 6 7
TOTAL:	_____	_____

Leadership Skills	Skill Level	Interest Level
1. Lead a team and facilitate a vision for a common goal	1 2 3 4 5 6 7	1 2 3 4 5 6 7
2. Identify a need or opportunity	1 2 3 4 5 6 7	1 2 3 4 5 6 7
3. Persuade others to buy in and participate	1 2 3 4 5 6 7	1 2 3 4 5 6 7
4. Develop course of action and innovative solutions	1 2 3 4 5 6 7	1 2 3 4 5 6 7
5. Motivate others to achieve goals	1 2 3 4 5 6 7	1 2 3 4 5 6 7
6. Identify/manage others skills/abilities to achieve results	1 2 3 4 5 6 7	1 2 3 4 5 6 7
7. Take risks; be decisive	1 2 3 4 5 6 7	1 2 3 4 5 6 7
TOTAL:	_____	_____

Creativity Skills	**Skill Level**	**Interest Level**
1. Use creativity, imagination and design skills	1 2 3 4 5 6 7	1 2 3 4 5 6 7
2. Conceptualize ideas, strategies and solutions	1 2 3 4 5 6 7	1 2 3 4 5 6 7
3. Use artistic ability at work	1 2 3 4 5 6 7	1 2 3 4 5 6 7
4. Use creativity to solve a problem	1 2 3 4 5 6 7	1 2 3 4 5 6 7
5. Express ideas and creative images through art	1 2 3 4 5 6 7	1 2 3 4 5 6 7
6. Think "outside the box"; looks for new ways	1 2 3 4 5 6 7	1 2 3 4 5 6 7
7. Use technology to create solutions	1 2 3 4 5 6 7	1 2 3 4 5 6 7

TOTAL: _____ _____

Administrative Skills	**Skill Level**	**Interest Level**
1. Communicate well with people at various levels	1 2 3 4 5 6 7	1 2 3 4 5 6 7
2. Organize or adapt office technology and software	1 2 3 4 5 6 7	1 2 3 4 5 6 7
3. Track progress of projects	1 2 3 4 5 6 7	1 2 3 4 5 6 7
4. Work within budget and deadlines	1 2 3 4 5 6 7	1 2 3 4 5 6 7
5. Ability to be flexible and level-headed during a crunch	1 2 3 4 5 6 7	1 2 3 4 5 6 7
6. Oversee office communications	1 2 3 4 5 6 7	1 2 3 4 5 6 7
7. Identify and purchase necessary office supplies	1 2 3 4 5 6 7	1 2 3 4 5 6 7

TOTAL: _____ _____

Financial Skills	**Skill Level**	**Interest Level**
1. Demonstrate strong math skills	1 2 3 4 5 6 7	1 2 3 4 5 6 7
2. Ability to maintain accurate financial records	1 2 3 4 5 6 7	1 2 3 4 5 6 7
3. Understand accounting functions and procedures	1 2 3 4 5 6 7	1 2 3 4 5 6 7
4. Compile data and analysis	1 2 3 4 5 6 7	1 2 3 4 5 6 7
5. Create spreadsheets and charts for presentation	1 2 3 4 5 6 7	1 2 3 4 5 6 7
6. Forecast and estimate expenses and income	1 2 3 4 5 6 7	1 2 3 4 5 6 7
7. Ability to identify/present pertinent financial information	1 2 3 4 5 6 7	1 2 3 4 5 6 7

TOTAL: _____ _____

Building/Mechanical Skills	**Skill Level**	**Interest Level**
1. Assemble and install technical equipment	1 2 3 4 5 6 7	1 2 3 4 5 6 7
2. Build a structure, follow proper sequence	1 2 3 4 5 6 7	1 2 3 4 5 6 7
3. Use hand coordination with tools	1 2 3 4 5 6 7	1 2 3 4 5 6 7
4. Knowledge of plumbing or electrical equipment	1 2 3 4 5 6 7	1 2 3 4 5 6 7
5. Master physical skills	1 2 3 4 5 6 7	1 2 3 4 5 6 7
6. Landscape and farm	1 2 3 4 5 6 7	1 2 3 4 5 6 7
7. Use scientific or medical equipment	1 2 3 4 5 6 7	1 2 3 4 5 6 7

TOTAL: _____ _____

List your top 5 Skill Categories.

1. _____

2. _____

3. _____

4. _____

5. _____

List your top 5 Interest Categories.

1. _____

2. _____

3. _____

4. _____

5. _____

MY VALUES INVENTORY

Next, examine your **values**, or the qualities you need and want in a work environment to feel motivated. There are no right or wrong answers! The Values Inventory will help you determine the work environment that is right for you.

Think back to your work experiences, internships and school experiences. Rate the following work values based on their importance to you. Be honest. Because there are no right or wrong answers, you will find this section more beneficial if you answer how you really feel. Circle the appropriate score.

A score of 7 = very important to have
A score of 1 = not at all important to have

Add your scores at the end of each section.

Working on My Own	Score
1. Work independently with little supervision	1 2 3 4 5 6 7
2. Work on individual assignments rather than group projects	1 2 3 4 5 6 7
3. Structure my own work and set my own goals	1 2 3 4 5 6 7
4. Spend my free time based on what I want to do as opposed to going along with the crowd	1 2 3 4 5 6 7
TOTAL:	_____

Using My Creativity	Score
1. Use my creative talents during the day	1 2 3 4 5 6 7
2. Be able to freely express my ideas	1 2 3 4 5 6 7
3. Look for new ways of doing things	1 2 3 4 5 6 7
4. Solve difficult problems creatively	1 2 3 4 5 6 7
TOTAL:	_____

Problem Solving (challenge)	Score
1. Thrive on solving a difficult problem	1 2 3 4 5 6 7
2. Enjoy conquering "the impossible"	1 2 3 4 5 6 7
3. Look for assignments that challenge me	1 2 3 4 5 6 7
4. Like to engage in complex and demanding tasks	1 2 3 4 5 6 7
TOTAL:	_____

Money	Score
1. Want the "good life"	1 2 3 4 5 6 7
2. Have a dependable income	1 2 3 4 5 6 7
3. Have potential for unlimited income	1 2 3 4 5 6 7
4. Live on my own, financially independent	1 2 3 4 5 6 7
TOTAL:	_____

Helping Others	Score
1. Help others directly	1 2 3 4 5 6 7
2. Feel that my work is making a difference	1 2 3 4 5 6 7
3. Feel needed by others	1 2 3 4 5 6 7
4. Give back; make the world a better place	1 2 3 4 5 6 7
TOTAL:	_____

Influence/Power	Score
1. Have influence over others	1 2 3 4 5 6 7
2. See the positive results of my efforts	1 2 3 4 5 6 7
3. Be able to persuade people to change opinions	1 2 3 4 5 6 7
4. Manage and be responsible for large projects or assignments	1 2 3 4 5 6 7
TOTAL:	_____

Achievement	Score		**Recognition**	Score
1. Advance to a high-level position quickly	1 2 3 4 5 6 7		1. Have a good job title and status	1 2 3 4 5 6 7
2. Develop my level of knowledge through hard work	1 2 3 4 5 6 7		2. Work for a well known and well respected organization	1 2 3 4 5 6 7
3. Accomplish my objectives	1 2 3 4 5 6 7		3. Be recognized by others	1 2 3 4 5 6 7
4. See results	1 2 3 4 5 6 7		4. Be respected by my peers for my effort and results	1 2 3 4 5 6 7
TOTAL:	_____		**TOTAL:**	_____

People Skills	Score		**Routine/Structure**	Score
1. Do my best work when working with other people	1 2 3 4 5 6 7		1. Prefer to have regular hours and predictable work	1 2 3 4 5 6 7
2. Enjoy working with others toward common goals	1 2 3 4 5 6 7		2. Prefer to do work where tasks are clear	1 2 3 4 5 6 7
3. Prefer working on a group project rather than on an individual assignment	1 2 3 4 5 6 7		3. Want to modify my job or schedule only when necessary	1 2 3 4 5 6 7
4. Enjoy working and studying with diverse personalities	1 2 3 4 5 6 7		4. More comfortable working with the same people everyday	1 2 3 4 5 6 7
TOTAL:	_____		**TOTAL:**	_____

Expression of Ideas	Score		**Development**	Score
1. Voice my ideas at work	1 2 3 4 5 6 7		1. Work in a job which has a defined career path	1 2 3 4 5 6 7
2. Demonstrate my unique talents at work	1 2 3 4 5 6 7		2. Have the opportunity for professional skill training	1 2 3 4 5 6 7
3. Have a job that I can change as my life changes	1 2 3 4 5 6 7		3. Have the ability to further my education	1 2 3 4 5 6 7
4. Be myself in the work environment	1 2 3 4 5 6 7		4. Be part of an industry that requires on-going learning	1 2 3 4 5 6 7
TOTAL:	_____		**TOTAL:**	_____

Now, score your results by adding up the numbers you have given to each value.

- List your top five Values in order of priority

1. _____

2. _____

3. _____

4. _____

5. _____

ALL ABOUT ME

Now, put it all together. Go back to each of the questionnaires you have completed. Transcribe the information listed below.

My Top Five Skills

1. _____

2. _____

3. _____

4. _____

5. _____

My Two Lowest Skills

1. _____

2. _____

My Top Five Interests

1. _____

2. _____

3. _____

4. _____

5. _____

My Top Five Values

1. _____

2. _____

3. _____

4. _____

5. _____

IDENTIFYING YOUR INTERESTS

Identifying how you like to spend your free time can help you narrow down what industry or field you would like to pursue. For example, someone with a degree in English who is pursuing an editing job may have an outside interest in cooking. That person will most likely be more satisfied with their career if they are working as an Editor for a publisher focusing on the cooking industry. They may not be as happy if they were editing a fishing magazine. This worksheet will help you to start thinking about your outside interests.

What do you like to do in your spare time?

What school subjects and organizations interest you the most?

What are your favorite movies, television shows, web sites?

What types of books, magazines, or newspapers do you like to read?

Review what you've written above. Write down three main areas of interest. Keep these in mind as you are researching various career opportunities and industries.

1. _____

2. _____

3. _____

THE RESEARCH PHASE

Now that you have a strong sense of your skills, interests, and values, it's time to see how this information "translates" into a job. A job or career choice can come from a specific occupation or from an environment or industry in which you're interested. There are many tools you can use to research your options, including:

- Personal contacts and networking
- Informational interviews
- On-line research

Keep in mind that the research process is not a linear one. That is, as you are researching job titles, you may also discover industries and/or potential employers that interest you. For example, you may start off looking for a position which uses your interpersonal and problem solving skills. As you research various job titles, you may find that a specific industry would appeal to you based on your interests. The important thing to remember is to keep an open mind to as many possibilities as you can. Your goal during the research process is to find out as much information as you can about a number of job titles and industries to determine where you want to focus your efforts.

As you are researching various careers, make sure your top skills and interests correlate to the jobs you're researching. As you're researching various industries, review your Values Assessment and your Interest list. Keep these in mind as you're setting your goals regarding the industries you wish to pursue.

At the end of this process, you will have identified one or more job titles, industries, and companies on which you will focus your job search.

The first step in researching various jobs is to ask people who know you for suggestions regarding the best career fit for you. From there, you may want to conduct some informational interviews to learn the realities of a job or company from people who already do the work. In this section, we will explore the benefits of these research tools, as well as how to use them.

Before you conduct this type of research, you will need to introduce yourself to potential contacts. Remember, **_every contact you make is an opportunity_.** Use the chart below to build your first commercial. This is a quick introduction to anyone you meet. It will tell them who you are and what you are looking for.

➤ Review this template and in the third column, write your commercial.

COMPONENTS	EXAMPLE	COMPLETE YOURS HERE
Your name	Jennifer Smith	
A recent grad of	Main College with a degree in economics	
I'm looking for: information, ideas, contact name or job lead	I'm looking for information about the financial services field.	
I am interested in this industry because...(you need a specific reason why you are interested)	I am interested in this industry because I did an internship at ABC Company and I really enjoyed the pace.	
Ask specific questions (ie, information about a particular industry or advice on how to pursue jobs in that industry.)	How would you recommend I learn more about entry level opportunities in the industry?	
Thank the person verbally and send a follow up email.	Thank you. I will plan to call John Adams at XYZ Company. May I use your name as a reference point?	

Practice your commercial with 3 friends or family members.

PERSONAL CONTACTS RESEARCH

Now you are ready to ask friends and family members for their advice regarding the best career options for you. Ask at least three friends and/or family members for suggestions. The best people to ask are usually the ones whose careers seem to interest you, or people who have had a fair amount of work experience.

Use your first commercial, which tells people who you are, what you are looking for, and why in 30 seconds or less.

WHO I CONTACTED	WHAT THEY SUGGESTED

INFORMATIONAL INTERVIEWS

An informational interview is a critical component of the research phase. It is a face-to-face meeting with someone in the field ou may be interested in. Your goal is to gather information about a position or an industry, or to get some job-hunting advice. It is not to ask for a specific job. Informational interviews can help you crystallize your career goals.

How to Conduct Informational Interviews

Choose the career field or company that interests you. Seek referrals from friends and family members. Call to introduce yourself (use your commercial), and ask for 15-20 minutes of that person's time at their place of work.

Prepare for the interview by researching the career field or company, and prepare some questions to ask. Here are some suggestions:

- How did you get started in this business?
- What made you choose XYZ Company?
- What do you like the most and least about this industry/company/job?
- What growth opportunities do you see in this field?
- What are the ideal education, background, and skills for success in this industry?
- What impresses you when interviewing candidates for entry-level positions?
- How do my skills and experiences match up?
- What advice can you give me as I pursue jobs in this field?
- Do you know of anyone else I could speak to or who might be looking for someone with my qualifications?

Arrive at the interview 10 minutes early and dress as if it were a job interview (see Rules of the Road, page 69). Ask the most important questions first and be sure to actively listen to the answers. Ask for additional names of people who could be of help in gathering more information.

After the interview, send a thank-you note to the person and evaluate the job or company using the worksheet on the following page.

INFORMATIONAL INTERVIEW EVALUATION WORKSHEET

This worksheet should be used in the informational interview process to help you evaluate potential career opportunities. Use it to write down your thoughts, questions and observations following the interview.

Career/Job Title: _____ Interviewee: _____ Date: _____

CATEGORY	OBSERVATION
What did you like the most about this industry, job or career track? *(What seemed challenging, rewarding or satisfying to you?)*	
What did you dislike?	
What did you learn about the daily tasks and responsibilities?	
What are the skills and experience required for this position/career? Are there training/career path opportunities?	
Are there gaps between your background and the job/career requirements?	
Who else should you talk to about this or related job fields?	

Are you interested in this career opportunity/industry/job?   Yes   No
(Circle one)

Copy of this page located in Forms section for photocopying if necessary.

ONLINE RESEARCH

Another great source of information is the internet. The following road map will show you how to research job opportunities online.

IF YOU ARE:	THEN YOU SHOULD:	WHERE DO I LOOK?
Not sure what careers are best suited for your major	Research career options for college major	**Research career options:** www.career.utk.edu/students/majors.asp
Not sure of careers that match your skills and interests	Research careers	**Match skills to occupations :** www.careeronestop.org **Conduct on-line research for career profiles:** www.bls.gov/oco/ www.collegegrad.com www.wetfeet.com/Careers---Industries.aspx
Interested in a specific career but not sure of the industry	Research specific industries	**Research specific industries:** www.collegegrad.com www.streamingfutures.com www.vaultreports.com
Sure about your career choice and industry but unsure of which companies you would fit in with	Identify companies that fit your lifestyle and work values	**Conduct on-line research for specific companies:** www.careerbuilder.com www.hotjobs.com www.monster.com www.vaultreports.com

The above websites were active as of the publication date.

JOB ANALYSIS

As you are researching jobs which interest you, use this sheet to record your findings.

Step One:

Fill in the job title/career in the first column – the skills and experience required for that job in the second column, the skills you have in the third column and the skills you're missing – the Gap – in the last column.

Step Two:

Fill in the additional information listed in the remaining columns.

JOB TITLE/CAREER	SKILLS AND EXPERIENCE REQUIRED	SKILLS AND EXPERIENCE I HAVE	GAP

KEY TASKS AND RESPONSIBILITIES	WORK ENVIRONMENT	CAREER & FINANCIAL OPPORTUNITIES	LIFESTYLE/LOCATION

Copy of this page located in Forms section for photocopying if necessary.

JOB ANALYSIS (cont.):

JOB TITLE/CAREER	SKILLS AND EXPERIENCE REQUIRED	SKILLS AND EXPERIENCE I HAVE	GAP

KEY TASKS AND RESPONSIBILITIES	WORK ENVIRONMENT	CAREER & FINANCIAL OPPORTUNITIES	LIFESTYLE/LOCATION

JOB ANALYSIS (cont.):

JOB TITLE/CAREER	SKILLS AND EXPERIENCE REQUIRED	SKILLS AND EXPERIENCE I HAVE	GAP

KEY TASKS AND RESPONSIBILITIES	WORK ENVIRONMENT	CAREER & FINANCIAL OPPORTUNITIES	LIFESTYLE/LOCATION

WHAT INDUSTRIES INTEREST YOU?

Choosing an industry that's right for you is critical. The work, environment, terminology, and the people you work with will vary greatly from one industry to another. Some questions you want to answer about each industry you are considering are:

1. What product or service does this industry offer?

2. What determines success in this industry?

3. What is the hiring outlook for this industry?

4. What type of talent does this industry need? Do I have some of these skills from past work experience or internships?

5. Does the subject matter of this industry relate to my favorite subjects in school or areas of interest?

6. What is the working environment like? Is it casual or professional? Does it line up with my work values?

INDUSTRY ANALYSIS

Listed below are some questions to assist with your research of various industries. Record your answers in the chart below.

Industry 1: _____

QUESTIONS TO ASK	ANSWERS
What product or service does this industry offer?	
What determines success in this industry?	
Is this industry hiring?	
What type of talent does this industry need?	
Do I have some of these skills from past work experience or internships?	
Does the subject matter of this industry relate to my favorite subjects in school or areas of interest?	
What is the work environment like? Does it line up with my work values?	

Copy of this page located in Forms section for photocopying if necessary.

INDUSTRY ANALYSIS (CONT.)

Industry 2: _____

QUESTIONS TO ASK	ANSWERS
What product or service does this industry offer?	
What determines success in this industry?	
Is this industry hiring?	
What type of talent does this industry need?	
Do I have some of these skills from past work experience or internships?	
Does the subject matter of this industry relate to my favorite subjects in school or areas of interest?	
What is the work environment like? Does it line up with my work values?	

INDUSTRY ANALYSIS (CONT.)

Industry 3: _____

QUESTIONS TO ASK	ANSWERS
What product or service does this industry offer?	
What determines success in this industry?	
Is this industry hiring?	
What type of talent does this industry need?	
Do I have some of these skills from past work experience or internships?	
Does the subject matter of this industry relate to my favorite subjects in school or areas of interest?	
What is the work environment like? Does it line up with my work values?	

WHAT COMPANIES DO YOU WANT TO WORK FOR?

Now that you have an idea of the jobs you want and the industries that interest you, you need to identify which companies offer this position, are hiring, and appeal to you.

Networking, informational interviews, internships, and volunteering are the best ways to find great companies.

You can use the on-line tools listed on page 24, but you can also make good use of the following **job boards**. On these sites, you can search by job title or key word. Keep in mind that the actual titles of jobs can change by company, so read the descriptions within each posting.

www.monster.com
www.careerbuilder.com
www.hotjobs.com
www.collegegrad.com
www.craigslist.com
www.vaultreports.com

Other resources not to be overlooked are **newspapers and magazines**.

Once you've identified a list of potential companies, learn as much as you can about them through their website, blogs, print media, and current employees.

List companies and 3 reasons why you want to work for them here.

COMPANY NAME	REASON 1	REASON 2	REASON 3

Questions to Think About

What are the Company's key products & services?

How is this Company different from others in industry?

What are the Company's values and culture?

How are employees treated?

Are there opportunities for good experience, training, & growth?

Copy of this page located in Forms section for photocopying if necessary.

YOUR CAREER GOALS

It's time to put all of your research together. The research you've done up until this point will enable you to set your career goals.

Over the next couple of pages, you will write your short- and long-term career goals.

Long-Term Career Goals

The first step is to establish your long-term career goals, or where you want to be in five years. Even if you are still a bit unclear on this, it's important to set a long-term goal.

Why?

It's much easier to determine what your next steps should be when you have a long-term goal. For example, when you were in college, you had to declare a major. You took a number of different courses which eventually lead to your major and degree. Setting a long-term career goal is very much the same process. Determining where you want to be in five years will help you identify the jobs you will pursue now. These jobs will help you develop the skills you need to attain your long-term career goal.

> **For example:** *My long-term career goal is to go into Pharmaceutical Sales and Business Development.*

Short-Term Job Goals

Your short-term job goals are the jobs you will pursue now, the ones that will help you attain your long-term goal. You may have more than one short term goal depending on the job market, the hiring outlook for the career you have chosen, and your background. The jobs to focus on in your short-term goals are ones where you will have an opportunity to learn more about the industry and develop the skills needed to achieve your long-term goal.

As you are setting your short-term job goals, it's important to keep your options open and be flexible.

Why?

You know your long-term career goals. If the job market is tight, you may not be able to get the job that is your first choice. Determine a variety of job options which will eventually lead you to your long-term goal. Some short-term job goals may get you there more quickly; however, the goal is to get there. It's important to keep in mind that you will learn and develop skills in every job you have.

RANK YOUR SHORT-TERM CAREER GOALS

Short-term Job Goal A is your desired job which is most closely linked to your long-term career goal.

Short-term Job Goal B targets a related job within your desired industry.

Short-term Job Goal C targets a position in an industry which works with or depends upon your desired industry.

For example:

Based on what I've learned about the pharmaceutical industry, the skills I will need are in-dustry knowledge, selling skills and product knowledge. The advice I've been given is to focus my search on Inside Sales positions, Customer Service, or Retail Sales of Medical Supplies. I've also been advised to target large pharmaceutical companies,hospitals and medical supply companies. I will have 3 short-term career goals.

Goal A:
Pharmaceutical Inside Sales at AstraZeneca, Genzyme and Johnson & Johnson.

Goal B:
Customer Service Position at AstraZeneca, Genzyme, Mass General Hospital, Lahey Clinic.

Goal C:
Retail Sales position at MPS Medical Supply Company, ALCO Sales or Insurance Sales.

EXAMPLE OF LONG- AND SHORT-TERM CAREER GOALS

1. **Long-term career goals identify where you want to be in 5 years.**

2. **Set a range of prioritized short-term goals:**
   a. Goal A is your desired job, directly linked to long-term goal
   b. Goal B targets a related job within your desired industry
   c. Goal C targets an entry level position which works with or depends on the desired industry

3. **List plans to fill background gaps.**

LONG-TERM CAREER GOAL
Pharmaceutical business development

SHORT-TERM JOB GOAL A	TARGET EMPLOYERS
Pharmaceutical sales position	AstraZeneca Genzyme Johnson & Johnson

SHORT-TERM JOB GOAL B	TARGET EMPLOYERS
Pharmaceutical customer service position	AstraZeneca Genzyme
Receptionist/administrative role in a medical facility	Mass General Hospital Lahey Clinic

SHORT-TERM JOB GOAL C	TARGET EMPLOYERS
Retail sales position	MPS Medical Supply ALCO Sales
Insurance sales	Aetna Cigna

BACKGROUND GAP	HOW I WILL FILL THE GAP
Knowledge of pharmaceuticals	Attend a one-day conference
Sales skills	Webinars or certified sales training

YOUR CAREER GOALS - Write your short- and long-term career goals

1. **Identify your long-term career goals or where you want to be in 5 years.**

2. **Set a range of prioritized short-term goals:**
   a. Goal A is your desired job, directly linked to your long-term goal
   b. Goal B targets a related job within your desired industry
   c. Goal C targets an entry level position which works with or depends on the desired industry

3. **List plans to fill background gaps.**

LONG-TERM CAREER GOAL

SHORT-TERM JOB GOAL A	TARGET EMPLOYERS

SHORT-TERM JOB GOAL B	TARGET EMPLOYERS

SHORT-TERM JOB GOAL C	TARGET EMPLOYERS

BACKGROUND GAP	HOW I WILL FILL THE GAP

SKILLS DEVELOPMENT PLAN

Now that you know which direction your career will take, you need to think about experiences you can pursue to build your resume.

> *For example,* if your career goal is to go into a management role, you will need specific leadership experiences to be considered for the job. Or, if you want to go into international business, you will need foreign language skills.

Take a few minutes to think about how you will build your resume to accommodate your goals and write down some ideas. This chart can get you started. The Activity section on the chart below should include specific steps you can take to develop the skills you will need. Examples of Activities are internships, temporary work, part-time work, or volunteering.

SKILL	ACTIVITY	DATE TO COMPLETE BY
Leadership: • Takes responsibility • Organized • Achieves results		
Communication skills: • Verbal • Written • Computer		
Business skills: • Economics, finance • Sales or marketing experience		
Foreign language skills		
Teamwork: • Team Player • Communication • People Skills		
Other		

Congratulations! You have now set career goals and determined what skills you will need to develop your long-term goals. Now it's time to learn how to articulate your skills in an interview situation.

PREPARE MYSELF

"Many employers reported that students...have poor communication skills...and are unable to articulate how what they have done relates to/contributes to the position they are seeking."
—NACE Job Outlook 2006

The next phase in your job search is called the "Prepare Myself" stage. It's important to make sure you're comfortable articulating what you want to do and why it will be a good fit for you. As you work through this chapter, you will also sharpen your interviewing skills as well as learn the "Rules of the Road" to successfully present yourself. At the end of this stage, you will be ready to interview with confidence.

THE FLOW OF PREPARE MYSELF

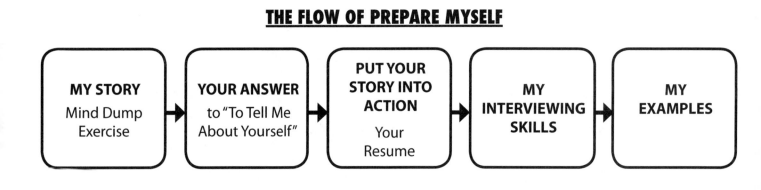

MY STORY
Mind Dump Exercise

YOUR ANSWER
to "To Tell Me About Yourself"

PUT YOUR STORY INTO ACTION
Your Resume

MY INTERVIEWING SKILLS

MY EXAMPLES

MY STORY

First, we begin with You. The "My Story" section, will help you think about your past experiences to see how they fit into your career goals.

In your interviews, you will most likely be asked the question, "Tell me about yourself". When you have finished this section, you will be able to clearly and concisely articulate how your past experience supports your job goals. In order to begin this process, you need to do a "mind dump". That is, write down everything you have done in your past, from selected accomplishments to learning experiences. It might be a time when you excelled at a project or it might be when you failed but were faced with a great learning opportunity. Include experiences that are academic in nature as well as work-related, family-oriented or social. Try not to limit yourself.

Remember, the people who get the jobs are the ones who are also thinking about what the employers are looking for—what type of candidate will they hire?

As you're working on this, keep in mind the top 10 personal qualities/skills employers want: *(The skills listed below are reported by the National Association of Colleges and Employers Job Outlook Survey):*

1. Verbal and Written Communication Skills
2. Honesty and Integrity
3. Interpersonal Skills
4. Strong Work Ethic
5. Teamwork Skills
6. Analytical Skills
7. Motivation and Initiative
8. Flexibility and Adaptability
9. Computer Skills
10. Detail-oriented

MY STORY - MIND DUMP EXERCISE

You can begin the mind dump exercise a number of different ways. Some people prefer to make a list of everything they've ever done in chronological order. Some people like to make a mind map, and some just like to start writing and see what they come up with. Mind mapping or making a list helps make sure you don't miss anything.

EXAMPLE OF A CHRONOLOGICAL LIST

High School	College
played violin	financed majority of education
swim team	worked part time at local pizza shop
student government treasurer	started up a study group for economics class
class steering committee	fundraising on college phone bank
summer camp counselor	summer jobs – general office work for ad agency
part time job at local ice cream shop	studied abroad in France

---

EXAMPLE OF A MIND MAP

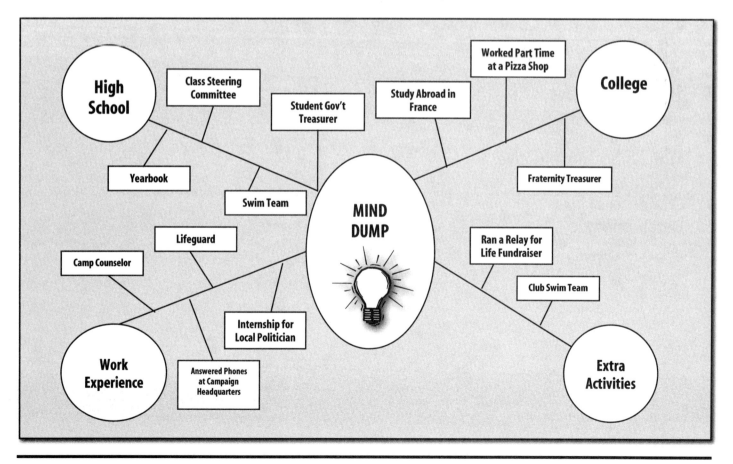

EXAMPLE OF A MIND DUMP EXERCISE

If you think an activity wasn't important or remarkable, think again about what you did. For example, you may have done a semester abroad program just like many college students. But maybe it wasn't like everyone else's.

"Jennifer" is a student who thought her semester abroad was a typical experience until she really described what she did. She chose to do a program which was not offered through her college, so she developed an outline for the classes she would take and her living arrangements, which included living with a family who spoke no English. In order to do this study abroad program, she needed to present her request to a panel of professors and administrators. Her request was approved, and she went abroad. She completely immersed herself in the culture, took classes which were dramatically different than what she was used to, and developed a strong friendship with her host family. She thought none of this was a big deal.

What skills do you think she needed to have in order to create this travel abroad program?

What skills do you think she gained from this experience?

To start, she shows that she takes initiative, is persuasive, and a risk-taker. She knows what she wants, and she not only goes after it, she presents her case professionally and takes what is now considered a fairly common program and turns it into an even better educational experience. She also shows perseverance and the ability to adapt to new environments.

She didn't realize the skills she had until she looked at her experience like an employer would.

MIND DUMP EXERCISE

- Use the space below to write down everything you've done.
- Write without limits using brainstorming tools that work for you.
- Then, using a yellow highlighter, mark those experiences which support your career goals.

WHAT IS A "MIND DUMP"?

Empty your head of all related experiences.

Write down everything you've done without limits:

- Projects
- Times you've excelled
- Times you've failed
- Challenges
- Obstacles

THINGS TO JOG YOUR MEMORY...

- Work experience
- Academics
- Honors, GPA
- Team projects
- Volunteer activities
- Awards
- Leadership activities
- Extra-curricular activities
- Creative activities
- Speeches
- Self-finanaced education
- Sports

NACE TOP 10

- Verbal and written communication skills
- Honesty and integrity
- Interpersonal skills
- Strong work ethic
- Teamwork skills
- Analytical skills
- Motivation and initiative
- Flexibility and adaptability
- Computer skills
- Detail oriented

"TELL ME ABOUT YOURSELF"

Now, let's focus on the answer to the most commonly asked interview question, **"Tell me about yourself".** Not only is this question commonly asked in interviews, it can a so be used as the basis for cover letters. This question can be asked in many different ways and is typically the first question which an interviewer asks. Some examples are:

"Why are you here today?"
"Tell me about your experience so far."
"What can I do for you?"

Use the information from your Mind Dump to write your story/answer.

It should be chronological and should relate to the job titles you've identified in your goals. As you're telling your story, try to relate your past experience to skills that apply to jobs you'll be interviewing for, as well as how you will contribute to the position.

This should be no more than 2-3 minutes spoken and should be conversational in nature.

> **Example:** *This candidate is interviewing for an entry level position in a non-profit organization which supports women's rights.*
>
> "My name is Mary Smith. I graduated from ABC University with a degree in women's studies. I started at ABC with a major in environmental science. At the time, I was passionate about the environment. I even completed an environmental internship in the Bahamas while I was in high school.
>
> But then, two things happened. First, I realized I was more interested in environmental policy as opposed to science. Second, I took an elective that addressed women's rights. A light went on for me. I've always supported women's rights, but this particular elective really hit home. I couldn't believe that women's rights were still an issue in this day and age. I switched my major to women's studies and, as my resume indicates, I have a lot of experience working on behalf of women. As you can see, I have worked as an advocate for abused women with the local community and legal system. I also provided counseling over the phone for underprivileged women. Even my experience teaching skiing has given me skills on how to work with different types of people.
>
> I am here today because I believe that my passion for women's rights as well as my experience in non-profit organizations will be beneficial to your organization."

YOUR ANSWER

Write your answer to the question "Tell me about yourself" in the space below. Make sure your answer sounds conversational.

_____

_____

_____

_____

_____

_____

_____

_____

_____

_____

_____

_____

_____

_____

_____

_____

_____

_____

_____

_____

_____

_____

_____

_____

_____

_____

YOUR ANSWER (CONT.)

_____

_____

_____

_____

_____

_____

_____

_____

_____

_____

_____

_____

_____

_____

_____

_____

_____

_____

_____

_____

_____

_____

_____

_____

_____

Practice this with 3 friends or family members.

PUTTING YOUR STORY INTO ACTION

Now, let's put your story into action. The first thing most people do when they begin a job search is to write a **resume**. In fact, you probably already have one. But, without spending the time to research yourself and potential jobs that fit you, it's very hard to capture the "you" on paper that will fit the jobs for which you'll be interviewing.

When drafting your resume, you need to use your personal information, or the result of your work writing "My Story".

You also need to use "keywords". Keywords or industry buzzwords are words that are specific to each job and are the words that are used in a company's resume database search engine. You can find these words in job descriptions posted with on-line job boards. Recruiters and hiring managers perform keyword searches on resume databases to obtain the most qualified applicants. If you don't use the right words, your resume could be passed over in spite of your qualifications.

> Some examples of keywords include: sales, accountant, customer service, finance, help desk, clerical, accounts payable. There are as many keywords as there are job types!

Where can you find key words?
Check job advertisements for your ideal position, employer websites and government job descriptions (Occupational Outlook Handbook: www.bls.gov/oco)

List 2-3 keywords for your goals here.

_____

_____

_____

_____

_____

COMPONENTS OF A RESUME

Name and Contact Information	• Check your email address; it must be a professional one! • Change the greeting on your voicemail and cell phone to a professional one!
Objective	• This is your career goal; include job type, industry, location • Include keywords!
Summary of Qualifications	• 1-2 sentences about why you are qualified for this position; what makes you unique? At the end, list 3-4 skills you excel at which relate to the job you're interviewing for • Remember your keywords!
Education	• Begin with degree, school, location, major and minor/concentration • List any academic awards, scholarships or certifications received • If you financed any part of your education, insert it here
Related Experience	• List any experience you have that supports the skills listed in the qualifications summary and the job for which you are interviewing: paid, unpaid, volunteer work, internships, etc. (put the dates on the right; title on the left) • Use action words to describe your work (See page 51-52 for a sample list of action words you can use.) • List specific accomplishments, quantify results if possible
Other Activities	• List other activities which support your "unique" factor but may not directly support the job for which you are interviewing. (Examples: community service, scouts, foreign language skills, travel, computer/technical skills)
References	• "Available upon request"

The following page is an example of a typical resume. Although there is no one "right" way to write a resume, this is a good basic format.

Jake A. Smith

456 Main Street
Boston, MA 02116

(617) 555-1234
jakeasmith@comcast.net

Objective: Marketing Research position in the financial services industry

Qualifications: Detail-oriented individual who can identify pertinent information and communicate it effectively
- ∞ Completed two marketing internships
- ∞ Facilitated presentation skills program for incoming freshmen
- ∞ Participated in a team to create welcome packages for transfer students

Education   ABC University   Boston, Massachusetts   June 2008

Bachelor of Science, Marketing; Concentration in economics and finance
Graduated cum laude
Self-financed 25% of education

Experience

XYZ Company   Boston, MA   2007
Marketing Intern
- ∞ Served as Marketing Assistant for Product Managers; supported the rollout of two new closed end mutual funds which generated $65m and $30m in assets, respectively.
- ∞ Processed and updated mailing list data for use in sales campaigns; sales teams improved their mailing responses by 10%.
- ∞ Coordinated broker visits designed to disseminate product information to increase sales. End result was a 3% increase in sales.

ABC University   Boston, MA   2006
Admissions Intern
- ∞ Worked in the admissions office to help attract transfer students to the school. Personally attracted 34 new students.
- ∞ Responsibilities included creating new students materials, giving tours, and working on the help line to answer questions

Other Skills and Activities

- ∞ Fluent in Spanish; Microsoft Word, Excel, and Power Point experience
- ∞ Member, Big Sister Organization; participated in Walk for Breast Cancer
- ∞ Interests include hiking, travel, exercise

References available upon request

ACTION VERBS

This is a list of words you can use to write an action-packed resume.

ACTION VERBS FOR RESUMES

Communication	Communication (cont.)	Creative	Financial	Counseling
Addressed	Outlined	Acted	Administered	Adapted
Advertised	Participated	Adapted	Adjusted	Advocated
Arbitrated	Persuaded	Began	Allocated	Aided
Arranged	Presented	Combined	Analyzed	Answered
Articulated	Promoted	Composed	Appraised	Arranged
Authored	Proposed	Conceptualized	Assessed	Assessed
Clarified	Publicized	Condensed	Audited	Assisted
Collaborated	Reconciled	Created	Balanced	Clarified
Communicated	Recruited	Customized	Budgeted	Coached
Composed	Referred	Designed	Calculated	Collaborated
Condensed	Reinforced	Developed	Computed	Contributed
Consulted	Reported	Directed	Conserved	Cooperated
Contacted	Resolved	Displayed	Corrected	Counseled
Conveyed	Responded	Drew	Determined	Demonstrated
Convinced	Solicited	Entertained	Developed	Diagnosed
Corresponded	Specified	Established	Estimated	Educated
Debated	Spoke	Fashioned	Forecasted	Encouraged
Defined	Suggested	Formulated	Managed	Ensured
Developed	Summarized	Founded	Marketed	Expedited
Directed	Synthesized	Illustrated	Measured	Facilitated
Discussed	Translated	Initiated	Netted	Familiarized
Drafted	Wrote	Instituted	Planned	Furthered
Edited		Integrated	Prepared	Guided
Elicited		Introduced	Programmed	Helped
Enlisted		Invented	Projected	Insured
Explained		Modeled	Qualified	Intervened
Expressed		Modified	Reconciled	Motivated
Formulated		Originated	Reduced	Prevented
Furnished		Performed	Researched	Provided
Incorporated		Photographed	Retrieved	Referred
Influenced		Planned		Rehabilitated
Interacted		Revised		Represented
Interpreted		Revitalized		Resolved
Interviewed		Shaped		Simplified
Involved		Solved		Supplied
Joined				Supported
Judged				Volunteered
Lectured				
Listened				
Marketed				
Mediated				
Moderated				
Negotiated				
Observed				

Leadership

Administered
Analyzed
Appointed
Approved
Assigned
Attained
Authorized
Chaired
Considered
Consolidated
Contracted
Controlled
Converted
Coordinated
Decided
Delegated
Developed
Directed
Eliminated
Emphasized
Enforced
Enhanced
Established
Executed
Generated
Handled
Headed
Hired
Hosted
Improved
Incorporated
Increased
Initiated
Inspected
Instituted
Led
Managed
Merged
Motivated
Navigated
Organized
Originated
Overhauled
Oversaw
Planned
Presided
Prioritized
Produced
Recommended
Reorganized

Leadership (cont.)

Replaced
Restored
Reviewed
Scheduled
Secured
Selected
Streamlined
Strengthened
Supervised
Terminated

Research

Analyzed
Clarified
Collected
Compared
Conducted
Critiqued
Detected
Determined
Diagnosed
Evaluated
Examined
Experimented
Explored
Extracted
Formulated
Gathered
Inspected
Interviewed
Invented
Investigated
Located
Measured
Organized
Researched
Reviewed
Searched
Solved
Summarized
Surveyed
Systematized
Tested

Organization

Approved
Arranged
Catalogued
Categorized
Charted
Classified
Coded
Collected
Compiled
Corrected
Corresponded
Distributed
Executed
Filed
Generated
Incorporated
Inspected
Logged
Maintained
Monitored
Obtained
Operated
Ordered
Organized
Prepared
Processed
Provided
Purchased
Recorded
Registered
Reserved
Responded
Reviewed
Routed
Scheduled
Screened
Submitted
Supplied
Standardized
Systematized
Updated
Validated

Teaching

Adapted
Advised
Clarified
Coached
Communicated
Conducted
Coordinated
Critiqued
Developed
Enabled
Encouraged
Evaluated
Explained
Facilitated
Focused
Guided
Individualized
Informed
Instilled
Instructed
Motivated
Persuaded
Simulated
Stimulated
Taught
Tested
Trained
Transmitted
Tutored

Technical

Adapted
Applied
Assembled
Built
Calculated
Computed
Conserved
Constructed
Converted
Debugged
Designed
Determined
Developed
Engineered
Fabricated
Fortified
Installed
Maintained
Operated
Overhauled
Printed
Programmed
Rectified
Regulated
Remodeled
Repaired
Replaced
Restored
Solved
Specialized
Standardized
Studied
Upgraded
Utilized

SOURCE:
Quintcareers.com

www.quintcareers.com/action_skills.html

YOUR RESUME

Create your resume using the information derived from "My Story" to make sure the "real" you shines through. Use the space below for your draft. Remember to use all applicable key-words and appropriate action words.

Name and Contact Information	
Objective	
Summary of Qualifications	
Education	
Related Experience	
Other Activities	
References	

REMEMBER TO....

- Be flexible!
- Your resume is not cast in stone.
- Revise it for different job opportunities.
- Keep your resume on a memory stick so you can change it as necessary.
- Always: proof, proof, proof!!
- A typo will get your resume moved to the garbage can fast!

❏ Research the job & include your keywords
❏ Remove your home address when posting online
❏ Keep your email address & phone number when posting online
❏ Limit your resume to one page
❏ Use a professional font
❏ Include your GPA if it's over a 3.0 on a 4-point scale
❏ Use spell check and grammar check
❏ Read your resume backwards to catch mistakes
❏ Ask at least 2 other people to proof your resume
❏ Before sending your resume to any employer, clean up your Facebook and LinkedIn pages. Review all of your pictures and comments to ensure they are appropriate. Assume that all employers will look for your profiles.

Remember, a resume is just one tool in the job search process. A resume alone will not get you a job. In many instances, it is a tool used to screen you out. There is no replacement for face-to-face contact.

MY INTERVIEW SKILLS

Now let's move on to the interview itself. You have prepared your "My Story". Your resume is done. Now, it's time to learn the flow of an interview and how to make it successful. Although interviews can vary, the following chart exemplifies the typical flow.

THE FLOW OF AN INTERVIEW

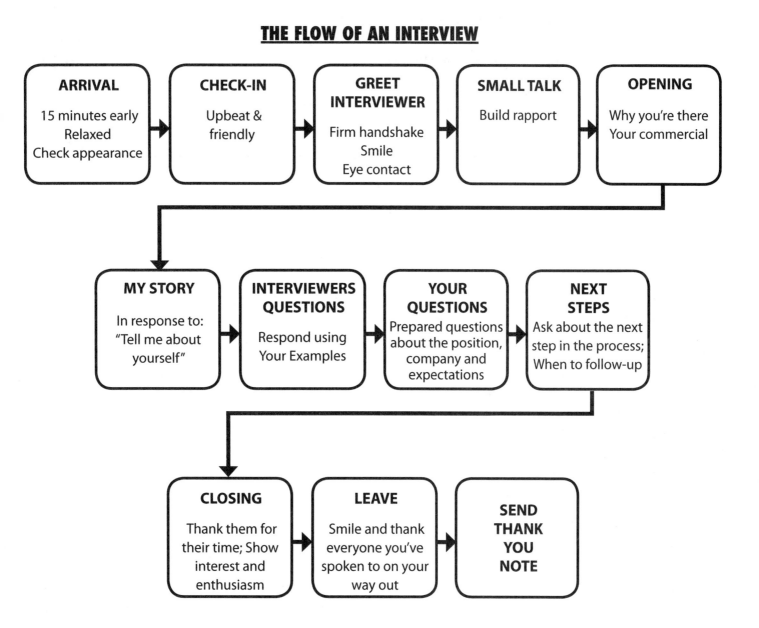

ARRIVAL

15 minutes early
Relaxed
Check appearance

CHECK-IN

Upbeat &
friendly

GREET INTERVIEWER

Firm handshake
Smile
Eye contact

SMALL TALK

Build rapport

OPENING

Why you're there
Your commercial

MY STORY

In response to:
"Tell me about
yourself"

INTERVIEWERS QUESTIONS

Respond using
Your Examples

YOUR QUESTIONS

Prepared questions
about the position,
company and
expectations

NEXT STEPS

Ask about the next
step in the process;
When to follow-up

CLOSING

Thank them for
their time; Show
interest and
enthusiasm

LEAVE

Smile and thank
everyone you've
spoken to on your
way out

SEND THANK YOU NOTE

THE INTERVIEW

As you are preparing for your interviews you will need to remember what employers are looking for as well as understand the flow of a typical interview.

Arrival

Arrive 15 minutes early to the location of the interview, but check-in as required, (reception desk or with the interviewer) only a minute or two before the designated interview time. Arriving at the location 15 minutes early will ensure that you don't walk in feeling late and rushed. It will give you an opportunity to use the restroom to check your appearance, wash your hands, check your teeth and relax.

Check-In

Be up-beat and friendly to everyone you encounter. You might just run into the President of the company in the parking lot or elevator. It's also important to make a good impression with the receptionist or administrative assistant.

Greet Interviewer

Smile! This is your first opportunity to connect with the interviewer. Maintain eye contact and greet them by their first name or however they introduce themselves. Shake their hand. A handshake is where you make a strong impression. Make sure you have a firm handshake, but don't crush them. Your hands should be clean and dry. If you're nervous, discreetly wipe your hands on your slacks/skirt before shaking.

Small Talk

Build rapport! The first 30 seconds is when you connect with the interviewer. People tend to hire people they like and with whom they connect. Be prepared with positive small talk like the weather or local sports.

Opening

You need to be prepared with an opening statement. State why you are there.

> **Example:**
> *It's so nice to meet you. I've been reading up on your company and I'm very excited to talk about this opportunity.*

Write your Opening in the space below.

THE INTERVIEW

Most interviews will begin with the question "Tell me about yourself". You have already prepared this answer in your "My Story". Remember, this is your opportunity to talk about the areas of your background which you want to highlight and that support the job requirements of the position for which you are interviewing.

- Your "My Story" is on page 46. Practice it out loud and make sure it answers the question, "Tell me about yourself". It's sometimes helpful to practice in front of a mirror or with friends.

There are a variety of other questions you need to be prepared for in an interview. They will be related to your skills, your college experience, your work experience, and what you want to do with your future. They can be asked in many different ways.

BEHAVIOR-BASED QUESTIONS

Behavior-based questions are very commonly used. Employers use behavior-based questions to see how you would act in particular situations. Some examples of behavior-based questions are:

- Tell me about a time when you had a difficult customer interaction.
- If you had to sell your ideas to someone more senior than you, how would you handle it?
- Give me an example of how you work on a team.
- Tell me about a time you experienced a big success.
- Tell me about a time you experienced a big failure.

Interviewers are looking for you to give examples of when you have used particular skills. They want to know how you will handle situations in the future. You want to show them that you already have the skills and qualities that they are looking for.

BEHAVIOR-BASED QUESTIONS

Interviewers are typically looking for specific skills when asking behavior-based questions. Your answers should include examples of these skills.

Your Communication Skills

- Verbal and non-verbal skills
- Your ability to convey your thoughts
- Your ability to speak clearly, concisely and keep their interest
- Your listening skills
- Your ability to answer the interviewer's questions
- If you go off on a tangent, it will appear that you didn't really listen to the question

Your Technical or Job Skills

- Convey that you have the skills to do the job
- Relate your answers to the job for which you are interviewing
- Show that you have "been there and done that"

Your Manageability Skills

- Show that you can work well with others
- Convey that you will be an employee who is easy to manage
- Share your eagerness to learn new skills
- Express your desire to grow within the organization
- Convey that you take direction easily
- Show that you understand their company's culture and will be successful in that environment

MY EXAMPLES

In order to prepare to answer behavior-based questions, you first need to compile a variety of examples of your work experience. These examples should include major accomplishments you've had in the work place or on large projects in school. They should be something you feel good about or that were great learning experiences.

The easiest way to pull these together is to go back to your Mind Dump on page 44. Choose 5 accomplishments or experiences that relate to the job you want.

> **Here's an example of an experience:**
> You raised money for breast cancer research and you're looking for a job in the health care industry.

> Do you see how these relate?

MY EXAMPLE – TURN IT INTO A STORY

It's important to prepare your "My Examples" so that you are able to use them when an interviewer asks you a behavior-based question. The ability to tell an interviewer about a time when you used a particular skill is just as challenging and important as being able to tell your "My Story". The interviewer needs to understand the story you're telling and how your skills enabled you to solve the problem. As you read on, you will see how you can structure your "My Examples" so that you give an overview of the experience, problem or project, then the details of the story and ending with the final result. On page 61 you will write your "My Examples" in the following structure:

MY EXAMPLE STRUCTURE

1. Summarize the experience/project

This should include what the project or experience was all about, what you were trying to accomplish, and who was involved.

> **Example:**
> *I provided sales and customer service at a sporting goods store. My goal was to make customers feel welcome and give them information about the products in which they were interested.*

2. Describe the obstacles or issues faced or great learning experiences

In every situation, there is something that makes the process more difficult. It could be working with a difficult team member, a change in a deadline date, or a time when you may have been faced with a project not in your area of expertise. These experiences show the interviewer that you will be able to handle difficult changes in their organization.

> **Example:**
> *A customer came in asking for a particular type and brand of kayak which we didn't carry in our store. I really wanted this customer to go away happy, so I used our computer to look up and see where he could find this kayak. It turns out that the only place to find this particular kayak was at a store in Denver, Colorado. I gave the customer the contact information and he called them and ordered it over the phone.*

3. Final Result

The Final Result is the end of the story. How did it end up? Was it successful? Why was it successful? What did you learn from the story? How does it relate to the job for which you are interviewing? If possible, use quantifiable results; that is, can you measure your success? Was it a satisfied customer who purchased more because of your service? Was it a specific increase or decrease in revenue/sales/customer satisfaction?

> **Example:**
> *I was so glad that I took the extra time to help this customer. He now comes to our store for all of his sporting good needs because of the outstanding service I gave him. It made me realize how important personalized customer service is, and I look forward to using this knowledge that I've gained in this position for your company.*

Structuring your examples this way will help you tell your stories in a clear and concise manner while highlighting your accomplishments and communication skills.

Use the following page to write down your examples which you will use during your interviews.

MY EXAMPLES - WRITE THEM!

Write the selected activities/experiences here. Remember the job requirements and tell a story.

SUMMARY/OVERVIEW	OBSTACLES/ISSUES/LEARNING	FINAL RESULT
Example 1		
Example 2		
Example 3		
Example 4		

The most important result of this exercise is the ability to tell each story with confidence. Practice your answers with 3 friends and family members.

INTERVIEW QUESTIONS

Interviewers and their questions will vary. No two interviews are exactly alike; in order to be successful, you need to be prepared for anything. Below is a list of typical interview questions. As you read them, think about your "My Examples" and how you can use them to answer these questions.

Typical Interview Questions

1. Tell me about yourself (and the variations on that question).
2. What are you most proud of from college?
3. How did you choose the college you attended?
4. Tell me about a difficult assignment/project/class. How did you handle it?
5. How did your education prepare you for your career?
6. Tell me about your leadership experience.
7. What personal accomplishments are you most proud of?
8. What do you want to do with your life?
9. How would you describe your ideal job?
10. Tell me about your career goals.
11. Describe a situation where you were successful.
12. Describe a situation where you failed and what you did about it.
13. What do you see yourself doing 5 years from now? 10 years from now?
14. How do you handle pressure?
15. How do you handle conflict?
16. Tell me about a time when you had to influence people you had no authority over.
17. When you're working on a team, what role do you typically play?
18. Tell me about a time when you played a leadership role on a team.
19. What was your GPA? Why wasn't it higher?
20. What are you looking for in a company?
21. What do you know about our industry?
22. What do you know about our company?
23. Why are you interested in this position?
24. Why are you interested in our company?
25. Are you willing to travel? Relocate?
26. What kind of salary are you looking for?
27. Why should I hire you over the next person who walks in my door?

Tricky Interview Questions/Comments

1. Why did you leave your previous job?
2. How much money do you want to make?
3. I'm sorry. I don't think this is a good fit. Thank you for your time.
4. Why weren't you working last summer?

EXAMPLES:

Describe a situation where you failed and what you did about it.

I was the head of the Student Government Association for my college. We were told to rewrite the constitution to reflect the fact that the school was going co-ed. Knowing we had a deadline of April 1st, we wrote what we thought should be the plan of action. What we failed to do was to get enough faculty "buy-in" of our ideas. What that meant was we missed the deadline. After we missed the deadline, we set up several meetings with various faculty members and then re-wrote the constitution. In the end we got their "buy-in" and support. I learned that in the future I need to have the support of everyone involved and if I'm not sure how to go about it, I need to confirm my process with someone above me.

When you're working on a team, what role do you typically play?

In most of my past work experience, I've found myself being the subject matter expert. For instance, when I was working on a team project for political science, we were researching cultural differences in communication styles in Japan. I had just been traveling in Japan and had a lot of information to offer the team. Though I would have enjoyed being the team leader, someone had already stepped into that role. By being flexible, I knew I could still contribute to the team as the subject matter expert. We got an 'A' on the project, and what I learned is that by focusing on the end result, I enjoyed contributing to a project regardless of the role I play on a team.

Why did you leave your last job?

In my last position as a Customer Service Representative, I was able to provide outstanding service to my customers. I really enjoyed working for a company that provided travel services; however, my real interest is in the creative writing and advertising field. I am hoping to use the skills I learned at this past position and bring them to this role as an Assistant Account Executive with your firm.

☑ Choose 5 questions from the previous page to respond to and write your answers on the following page. At least one should be a Tricky Question.

✏ MY ANSWERS TO 5 INTERVIEW QUESTIONS

Choose 5 interview questions from the list and write your answers here. Be sure to use your *My Examples* when answering the questions.

1. _____
_____
_____
_____

2. _____
_____
_____
_____

3. _____
_____
_____
_____

4. _____
_____
_____
_____

5. _____
_____
_____
_____

CRITICAL INTERVIEW QUESTIONS

The following questions may or may not be asked in all interviews; however, they are important questions to be prepared for. Even if you are not asked these questions, your answers will be important for you to bring up on your own at some point throughout the interview.

Complete the exercises below.

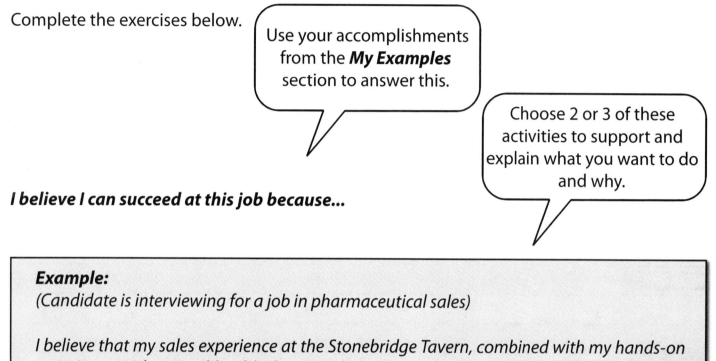

Use your accomplishments from the *My Examples* section to answer this.

Choose 2 or 3 of these activities to support and explain what you want to do and why.

I believe I can succeed at this job because...

> **Example:**
> *(Candidate is interviewing for a job in pharmaceutical sales)*
>
> *I believe that my sales experience at the Stonebridge Tavern, combined with my hands-on experience with mental health drugs at the Odyssey Home for Girls, makes me a strong candidate for this position.*

Your Answer:

_____

_____

_____

_____

_____

_____

_____

_____

_____

_____

You should hire me over the next person who walks through the door because...

> **Example:**
> I bring a strong work ethic to the job. As we discussed, when I worked at the Odyssey Home for Girls, I was faced with many difficult situations where I had to think on my feet and quickly resolve problems. I believe these skills will be an asset, as well as my desire to improve the quality of life for those with mental health issues.

Your Answer:

_____

_____

_____

_____

_____

_____

_____

_____

_____

_____

_____

_____

_____

_____

_____

_____

_____

_____

_____

_____

_____

_____

QUESTIONS FOR THE INTERVIEWER

It is important to show that you've done your homework and you're really interested in the positions for which you are interviewing. Go back to the Industry and Company Research section, pages 29-33. Prepare two questions about the job and company for which you're interviewing. As you're preparing these questions, also be prepared with statistical information about the company, such as:

• Size of the Company - number of employees, revenue, location sites
• History of the Company
• Recent news reports
• Product lines

Be prepared with questions that show you've done your research on:
• the Company
• the job

Examples:
What would the ideal person accomplish in this position?

In this position I understand I will be working with stocks and bonds. What are some of the challenges I will be faced with at year end? Will there be opportunities for additional projects because of this?

Your Questions:

1. _____

_____

_____

_____

_____

2. _____

_____

_____

_____

_____

NEXT STEPS AND CLOSING THE INTERVIEW

- When the interview ends, be prepared with a closing which ensures a follow-up conversation.
    - Match your closing to your personality, the position, and the interviewer.

- Express your interest in the job, and state your excitement to join their organization.

- Ask, "Is there anything in my background that I can explain further?"
    - What is your interview process?
    - What is the next step?
    - May I call you next week to follow-up?

CLOSING EXAMPLE:

Thank you so much for your time. I am very interested in this opportunity and feel that my summer internships at ABC Bank in the accounting department have given me the skills to transition into this position. I'm very excited about the opportunity to grow with this company. What is the next step in the process? or Is it okay if I follow up with you next Monday?

✏ **Write your closing below:**

_____

_____

_____

_____

_____

UPON LEAVING

- Thank the interviewer for his/her time and consideration
- Thank everyone you came into contact with while you're walking out

THANK YOU NOTE

- Send a thank-you email as soon as you get home
- Also send a hard-copy thank-you note

Review the completed exercises and practice them with at least 3 friends or family members. The more you practice, the more comfortable you'll become. Good luck!

RULES OF THE ROAD

Now that you know the flow of an interview, there are a number of "Rules of the Road" you should follow. Below is a checklist for presenting yourself, as well as how to prepare before the interview and rules for during the interview.

Present Yourself Checklist
❑ Wear a conservative 2-piece suit for men; for women, a white or pastel shirt/blouse or industry-appropriate attire
❑ Clean shoes
❑ Empty pockets
❑ For men: dark shoes and socks; conservative tie; get a haircut; no facial hair
❑ For women: no dresses, suits only; shoes with conservative heels; one set of earrings; one ring on each hand; minimal makeup, appropriate grooming (wax, pluck)
❑ Limited jewelry
❑ No visible piercings, tattoos - clean hair
❑ No cologne or perfume – assume people have allergies to it
❑ Use extra deodorant
❑ Try on your interview outfit 2 days in advance to make sure it fits, it's clean, and it's comfortable
❑ No sunglasses or gum

Before The Interview Check List
❑ Prepare company research
❑ Prepare questions for the interviewer – (page 67)
❑ Drive/travel to interview location before interview day
❑ If possible, go into office and notice how people are dressed
❑ Dress a step more professional than what employees are wearing
❑ Eat a good meal ahead of time
❑ Confirm your directions
❑ Give yourself extra time to get there
❑ Arrive 15 minutes early to the building
❑ Arrive at the interviewer's office no more than 5 minutes ahead of time
❑ Bring extra copies of your resume in your portfolio
❑ Bring a pen for taking notes

Arrival
❑ Don't walk in feeling late and rushed
❑ Use the restroom and feel relaxed - this will help you appear confident
❑ Check your appearance and wash your hands
❑ Notice the surroundings and look for employee publications, trade magazines, awards, etc.

Check-In
❏ Be upbeat and friendly with everyone you encounter – you never know who is going to be in the parking lot, elevator, or waiting area
❏ It's important to make a good impression with the receptionist or administrative assistant
❏ Tell him/her that you have an appointment or meeting – not an interview

Greet Interviewer
❏ Wait for the interviewer to come and get you
❏ Don't hover at his/her office door
❏ Smile! This is your first opportunity to connect with the interviewer
❏ Maintain eye contact
❏ Greet the interviewer by name
❏ Firm Handshake! This is where you make your first impression. Your handshake should be firm but don't crush their hand. Your hands should be clean and dry.

Small Talk
❏ The first 30 seconds is when you want to connect with the interviewer
❏ Begin building rapport!
❏ People tend to hire people they like and with whom they connect
❏ Be prepared with small talk: the weather or local sports are always safe topics, but keep it positive

Rules of the Road *During* the Interview
❏ Watch your body language – sit up straight and confident
❏ Use hands appropriately: if the interviewer doesn't talk with their hands, keep your hands still
❏ Be enthusiastic
❏ No gum
❏ Don't smoke cigarettes ahead of time
❏ Turn cell phone off
❏ Ask if you can take notes
❏ Vary your voice, use inflection to hold their attention
❏ Don't be afraid of a silence. Take your time to formulate your answers
❏ Don't use the word "but"; use "and" instead
❏ Don't swear
❏ Speak professionally, don't be too casual
❏ Sit up straight in the chair with good posture, shoulders back - This will relax you and make you appear comfortable and confident
❏ Don't lean on the interviewer's desk or invade his/her space
❏ Ask for the interviewer's business card
❏ Smile and enjoy yourself!

TYPES OF INTERVIEWS

There are several different types of interviews when you are looking for a job. Each has its own purpose and requires preparation on your part.

Informational Interviews

As stated in the first section of this book, an informational interview is a critical component in the job search process. See page 22 for preparation tips and suggested questions for informational interviews.

Job Interviews

Although you should be prepared to have at least two interviews at a company for most professional positions, there are times when one interview will land you the job. Remember, your interviews are the time to show what you're capable of; however, intangibles are also critical. Building rapport with your interviewer is very important.

Phone Screen

There are times when companies will conduct phone interviews. This type of interview is used to quickly screen people to determine who they will bring in for a face-to-face interview. They are usually conducted by a recruiter and differ from face-to-face interviews in one crucial way: there are no body language cues for you to pick up on. As a result, you need to use your voice patterns – highs and lows, enthusiasm, pauses – in addition to your background to sell yourself. Standing while speaking as well as smiling makes it easier to use inflection in your voice to convey your personality. You also need to listen carefully to the recruiter and concentrate on the tone of their voice so you can determine the flow of the interview. Your goal is to obtain a face-to-face meeting.

First Round Interview

The first face-to-face interview is used to assess your motivation and compatibility with the job and the organization. These interviews are typically conducted by a recruiter whose job it is to narrow down the applicants and refer the top candidates for a second interview. Your goal is to stand out from the crowd. Be mentally prepared to answer the question "Why should I hire you over the next person I meet?"

Second Interviews and Beyond

When you are referred for a second interview, it means you are being seriously considered for the position. Typically, the company has narrowed down their candidate pool to a small group of qualified candidates. The questions may become more technical in nature. Typically, the second interview is conducted by the hiring manager who wants to know how you can apply your education and past work experience to the job. Be prepared with "My Examples".

Of course, for all interviews, the Rules of the Road apply. In addition, a thank-you note should be sent within 24 hours of the interview. You should send an e-mail to everyone you met and follow it up with a hard-copy letter. You will find examples of thank-you notes in the next section.

Likeability Factor

In all interviews, a critical component to success is likeability. The term *likeability* is relatively new, but the concept isn't. If you are going to spend 40+ hours a week with someone, you want to like them. This same concept is true in hiring. We're not talking about a popularity contest. If a hiring manager is trying to make a decision between two highly qualified candidates, it is likely that they will hire the one they "like". You've probably heard the term "good-fit"—likeability is similar to good-fit, but it can be even more intangible. It has to do with how we connect with people. Throughout your interviews, one of your goals is to get the person who is interviewing you to "like" you. You do this through building rapport, showing confidence, and being in tune with what they are looking for. Remember, likeability is a two-way street. If you're interviewing at a company and you don't like the hiring manager or anyone else you meet, it's not the right fit for you.

You've just completed the **Prepare Myself** section. You've set your goals and you now know how to interview. Now it's time to plan and execute your job search. Where do you start? Well, the first thing you'll need to do is learn how to "sell" yourself.

WHAT DO YOU MEAN, I HAVE TO SELL MYSELF?

When you are looking for a job, you are selling yourself – your skills, your abilities and your experiences – to potential employers in exchange for payment or salary. Because the competition is tough, you need to approach this process like any sales person would: with the strong belief that your product – You – is the best available product on the market. You need to think like a sales person and be ready to ask for the "sale". In this case, the "sale" might be a contact name, information, a job interview, or, ultimately, a job. For some people, this comes naturally. If you are not one of those people, don't worry! The tools, tips and strategies in this chapter will help you.

In this section, you will learn how to sell yourself and how to plan and manage your job search.

SELL YOURSELF PROCESS FLOW

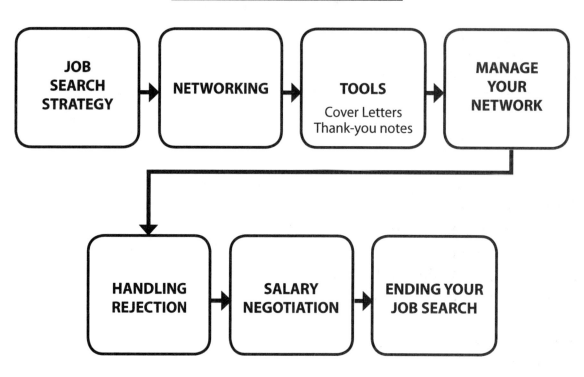

JOB SEARCH STRATEGIES

Create a Job Search Strategy that Works for You

As any sales person knows, you need to have a strategy or a plan to close the sale in the most efficient way. You want to make the best use of the time you spend looking for a job you want.

This section focuses on where the jobs are and how you can approach your job search with the highest degree of success.

Where are the Jobs?

You probably know people who have found jobs on the internet, through on-campus interviewing, or even through a job fair. But, you probably also know more people for whom these strategies did not work. If you want a job, you have to think like the employer. So, let's take a look at how employers typically fill jobs.

Hiring from within

Employers typically look internally to fill positions. Internal candidates are known quantities. They know the company, the culture and the policies. Many companies have a policy that requires that all open positions be posted internally before any external candidates are considered. Although it's difficult for college graduates to get a job this way, internships and temporary work within your target companies can help secure permanent work. It's also helpful to get to know someone who is on the inside to get a referral.

Personal Referral

Second, employers will ask a friend or business contact if they know of anyone who can fill the job. A personal referral is a great way to find a job. In fact, many companies sponsor employee referral programs which pay employees to refer someone to fill a job. And, in some cases, jobs are not even posted. They are simply "talked about".

Employment Agency

Companies at times will use employment agencies to fill their positions. Although this can happen, not many companies will pay a "finder's fee" for a young professional with limited experience.

Job Boards/Newspapers

Employers will typically use a variety of job boards or newspapers to help fill entry-level positions if they have a high number of job openings.

Reviewing resumes that come in unsolicited

Employers review resumes sent in to the company unsolicited. Companies vary on how they handle these resumes. Some automatically scan them into their recruiting database, and some have a junior recruiter review them.

With this in mind, let's look at how you can approach your job search.

JOB SUCCESS RATES BY SOURCE FOR YOUNG PROFESSIONALS

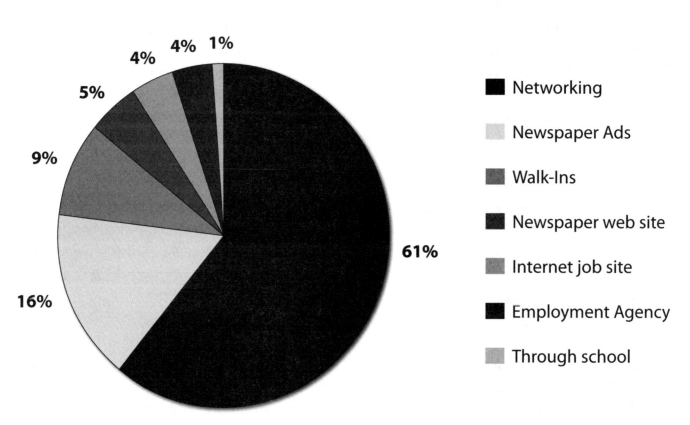

Source: Taylor Nelson Sofres Intersearch

Networking

Let's start with the most successful approach.

Networking is when you use your contacts and research to find the job that is right for you. At school, you were able to find out which cafeteria served the best food or which professors were the best in a particular course of study. Networking is the same thing applied to the working world. It works like this: you tell your friends, family, and friends of family what your goals are. (Use your commercial). Starting with the people on your list that you feel the most comfortable calling, ask your first contact, Contact "A", if they know anyone you can call to get more information. Send Contact A a thank-you note and call Contact "B". When you call B, use A's name as a referral. Contact B may give you more information or another name to call – Contact "C". Thank Contact B and follow up with the lead or suggestions they gave you. With each contact you make, you are closer to a job lead that's right for you.

The most important step in the process is follow-up! Keep all of your contacts informed of your progress. Act on any information or job lead that has been given to you.

Face-to-face networking can and should become part of your everyday life. We've already talked about how you will use it to contact friends and family, but you also need to become comfortable networking anywhere you go. When you go to a friend's party, there could be others who work in the industry in which you're looking. Ask your friend who will be there, then use your commercial in a casual, conversational way with anyone with whom you're talking. You can also use your networking skills at sporting events or shopping at the mall. Become comfortable making conversation with anyone you encounter.

This strategy has the highest success rate for finding a job, particularly one that is more meaningful because you are tapped into the known as well as the hidden job market. Studies have shown that networking has a success rate of 61% for young professionals. The success rate of networking increases to 80% to 85% as your career progresses.

On-Line Job Boards are one of the first places where most people start their job search. But as we saw, it is one of the last places an employer looks for qualified candidates. In fact, only posting your resume averages anywhere from a 4% to 10% success rate. *("What Color is Your Parachute", 2007)*

Newspapers, magazines and trade journals also post jobs. Although companies do fill jobs through print ads, the success rate ranges from 5% to 16%, depending on the type of role. Don't overlook the uses of newspapers and trade journals in your job search. Scanning the headlines each day will give you information on changes that are taking place in various companies. A company you are interested in may be hiring for other types of jobs. This at least shows that the organization is expanding and may mean future hiring within the area you are looking.

Employment Agencies are used when a company pays an outside recruiter to fill a position for them. Although not commonly used for entry level positions, they do have a use in a targeted job search. Meeting with professional recruiters is a great way to practice your interviewing and get feedback on your resume.

Job fairs are a great way to network and learn about different companies. Typically, job fairs are designed to "screen" as many people as possible quickly. It is a mechanism to collect resumes and get a quick "look see" of candidates. The recruiters who work at job fairs can see as many as 100 candidates in any given day, so it can be hard to be remembered.

Our recommendation for finding the job that is right for you is to plan your job search using a **targeted approach**. Use all job sources and allocate your time based on the success rates. For example, you would not want to spend more than 10% of your time surfing the job boards because the success rates don't support that strategy.

HOW DO I MAXIMIZE MY USE OF JOB SOURCES?

Networking:
❏ Prepare and use your commercial.
❏ Use the Networking Contact Info Sheet (located in the back of the book) to track all contact names, phone numbers, results, and follow up.
❏ Make 2-3 contacts per day.
❏ Email to introduce yourself, and follow up with a phone call.
❏ Call before 8:30a.m., at 12:00 – lunch time – or after 5:00p.m.
❏ If you get voicemail, leave a clear message and then follow up when you say you will.
❏ Persistence is critical! Be polite and clear, but don't be annoying.
❏ When you call, ask for 15 minutes of their time only.
❏ You are looking for ideas or information, not a job!
❏ At the end, ask: is there someone else you can suggest that I contact?
May I use your name?
❏ Always follow up immediately with a thank-you note and keep your initial contact in the loop.
❏ Remember, networking can and should happen all throughout your day wherever you are, i.e., social events, lunch with friends, family gatherings, shopping at the mall, etc.

Newspaper ads:
❏ Respond to the ones for which you are at least 50% qualified.
❏ If at all possible, be prepared to personally deliver your resume and cover letter to the company on Monday morning—the day after the ad was placed. Address it to the last person listed in the ad (if more than one person listed.)
❏ If it is a blind ad (only a post office box is written and no company name is given), be the first (Saturday night) or the last (Wednesday) to respond.
❏ Highlight a few (no more than 4) keywords on your resume with a yellow highlighter.
❏ Cover letter should have 2 columns: Job Requirements and My Qualifications.
❏ Find out who the hiring manager is.
❏ Follow up within one week.

Internet Job Boards:
❏ Double-check your resume. Make sure that your keywords match the job posting (to the extent that it represents you). Remove your mailing address.
❏ Don't just post your resume and wait. Find out who the hiring manager is and follow up by phone and snail mail.
❏ Always send (or better yet, hand deliver) an original copy of your resume to the company.

HOW DO I MAXIMIZE MY USE OF JOB SOURCES? (CONT.)

Employment Agencies:
- ❏ Get a referral from friends or family.
- ❏ Treat it like a real job interview.
- ❏ Recruiters are paid to fill a job. This can be good interview practice for you. Contact them when things on the job search are slow. They will usually agree to see you (especially if you have a reference), and it's a great confidence builder.
- ❏ It's your job to stay in touch with them!

Job Fairs:
- ❏ Research ahead of time what companies will be there and who you want to see.
- ❏ Learn about these companies ahead of time.
- ❏ Be prepared with your 30-second commercial, 2 open-ended questions to ask, and 2 copies of your resume for each company you wish to see.
- ❏ Be prepared to answer questions quickly.
- ❏ Take extra care of your appearance: you may have no more than 2-3 minutes with the recruiter, so appearance and presence will make the difference even more than in a typical 30-minute interview.
- ❏ Follow up: Leave a voice mail that day to thank the recruiter. Send a standard thank-you letter in the mail as well.

Getting Hired from Within:
- ❏ If there is one particular company you know you want to work for, consider trying to get some temporary work, an internship, or getting to know someone who works there now.

HOW TO WORK WITH AND AROUND RECRUITERS AND HR PROFESSIONALS OR...THE TWO-PRONGED APPROACH.

The question is typically asked, "Who should I try to get in touch with? A Recruiter or the Hiring Manager?"

What's tricky about this question is that every company's hiring policies can be different. At some companies, Human Resources/Recruiting is there only to make sure the paperwork is complete and their employees get paid. At other companies, the Human Resources/Recruiting staff may have more authority and all new hires have to go through them first. In that case, if you deliberately go around Human Resources/Recruiting, it will work against you. Part of your company research should be to determine what role Human Resources/Recruiting plays in the organization. You can simply ask your contacts who the most appropriate person to contact would be. If you are unsure, it's always best to contact both.

Recruiters and Human Resource Professionals are critical to you as a candidate. A Recruiter is typically the first person you will speak with when applying for a job. Even though they usually aren't the person who will make the hiring decision, you will need to interview with them. A Recruiter can be one of your best allies during the interview process. They're not only interested in knowing whether you are capable of doing the job you're interviewing for, but also how you fit within the organization. Your goal is to get the Recruiter to want to hire you. If a Hiring Manager is having a difficult time making a final decision, they may call the Recruiter for their thoughts. You want to be the one they recommend. If you are not the first-choice candidate, the Recruiter can present you to other Hiring Managers within the company.

TEMPORARY TO "PERM"

One approach that works well for young professionals is to obtain a temporary job in an organization and then convert that position to full time employment. "Temp-to-perm" works well for many reasons. First, you can try an organization to see first hand how it runs and how it treats its employees. You can also use that time to learn the organization's products, services and industry. This approach is especially useful if the organization is on your target list of employers. The company, on the other hand, can get a sense of who you are and what type of an employee you will be.

The first step in using this approach is to contact local temporary employment agencies. Be sure that your resume is in top shape and treat the encounter as you would a real interview. Understand that the recruiters typically have to fill requisitions quickly, so it's very important to make a great impression.

Be open to any and all assignments they may have and do whatever they ask of you to the best of your ability. Getting good feedback from the employer is the best way to get future assignments.

Not all temporary jobs can or will be converted to full-time positions, so keep your job search active while you are temping.

THE ROLE OF THE INTERNET

The internet has a critical role in your job search. First, you can use it to search for jobs on the various job boards. You can also use the various social media sites to network and find jobs. There are many sites available, but we recommend LinkedIn and Twitter. These sites are typically more professional than Facebook or MySpace. Jobs are posted on them, and you can also make contacts on there. Be sure to use them appropriately: post useful information which shows your commitment and knowledge, i.e., a pertinent blog or article. In addition, recruiters are using social networking websites to find candidates. Your profiles need to include keywords which reflect the job titles in which you are interested. As a reminder, refer back to page 48 for information regarding keywords.

Blogs are also useful. You can start a blog to show your expertise in your chosen field as well as comment on other blogs to raise awareness of who you are as a potential candidate.

> **For Example:** *One of our clients is an expert on professional sports clothing and uniforms. He wants to pursue a career in sports clothing design. He created a blog that talks about what various teams are wearing and the history of their uniforms. He now has a following.*

You can also set up a Google Alert account using the names of your targeted companies as the keywords. Each day, you will get an email which lists all current press about those companies. It's an easy way to stay informed.

As always, make sure all of your sites and profiles are clean and professional. Employers check these sites as part of their reference checking policies.

New networking sites are being created all the time. It's important to be aware of what's out there and which ones will be the most useful.

NETWORKING: EVERYONE YOU KNOW IS A CONTACT!

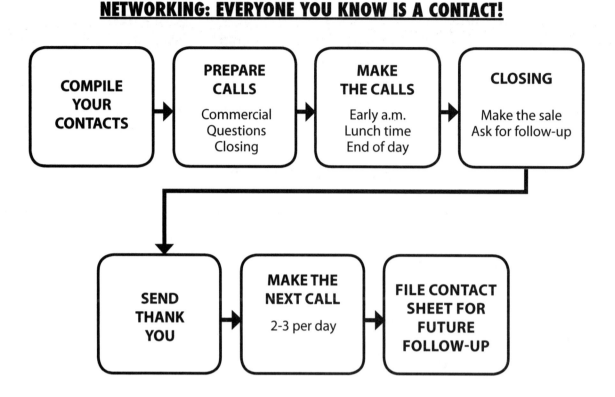

COMPILE YOUR CONTACTS → PREPARE CALLS — Commercial, Questions, Closing → MAKE THE CALLS — Early a.m., Lunch time, End of day → CLOSING — Make the sale, Ask for follow-up

SEND THANK YOU → MAKE THE NEXT CALL — 2-3 per day → FILE CONTACT SHEET FOR FUTURE FOLLOW-UP

Using your contacts improves your chances!!!
Friends
Family
Friends of Friends
Classmates
Teachers
Neighbors
Previous co-workers

Take a few minutes and begin your list of contacts. This will be a running list; keep adding to **it as you** progress through your job search.

CONTACT LIST

MY CONTACTS	HOW I KNOW THEM	WHERE THEY WORK

Copy of this page located in Forms section for photocopying if necessary.

YOUR FIRST CALL
Making that first call can be scary for some people. We recommend that you contact someone you know and are comfortable with for your first call.

Before you pick up the phone, think about what you want to get from the call. Is it a contact name? Is it information? Write down what you want to say. Remember the template:

Who you are	Good morning. My name is Jake Smith.
A recent graduate of...	I am a recent graduate of ABC University.
What you are looking for and why	I am looking for some information on potential opportunities in your industry. I have a background in biology, and several people have suggested I look into the biotech industry.
What you want from them	I was wondering if you can spend 15 -20 minutes with me some time next week so I can get your input on the industry and potential opportunities.
Close	Next Tuesday at 8:30 would be great. Thank you and I look forward to seeing you.
Follow up	Send your resume ahead of time for review. Thank your initial contact.

WRITE YOUR FIRST CALL:

Who you are	
A recent graduate of...	
What you are looking for and why	
What you want from them	
Close	
Follow up	

Practice it with at least 3 friends or family members.

MY COMMERCIAL, REVISED

Next, you need to **revise your commercial**. (Remember this? This was your original "commercial" on page 21.) Since you now know your objectives, it's time to expand your "commercial" into a 30-second commercial. You will use this commercial throughout your job search, when you're networking with friends, family, and job contacts, as well as on a job interview.

Let's review the key components of your commercial.

Who you are	Good morning. My name is Jake Smith.
A recent graduate of...	I am a recent graduate of ABC University with a degree in Communications.
What you are looking for: job type, industry, location (sound familiar? It's the verbal version of your career objective that's on your resume)	I am looking for an inside sales job in the advertising industry in the greater Boston area.
Why you are looking for it...	I have done two sales internships in an ad agency as well as some fund-raising for ABC University. I want to continue to use those skills as I move through my career.
Ask for something specific. **Be sure to plan ahead!**	Do you know of any job leads? Do you have a contact in that field? May I contact them?
Close	Can I use your name?
Thank the person	Thank you. I will keep you in the loop.
Next steps after the call	Write down the contact information on your "Contact Log". Call the contact you were referred to. Put the information in a binder/accordion file or an online calendar. Send an email to your original contact to let them know your current status. Complete your "Contact Log" sheet including both contact names.

MY COMMERCIAL, REVISED

Now, write your expanded commercial, using your career goal. It is similar to your networking call and can be used for a network call or in any conversation you have with people about your job search.

	WRITE YOUR COMMERCIAL HERE ↓
Who you are	
A recent graduate of...	
What you are looking for: **job type, industry, location** **(sound familiar? It's the verbal version of your career objective that's on your resume)**	
Why you are looking for it...	
Ask for something specific. **Be sure to plan ahead!**	
Close	
Thank the person	
Next steps after the call?	

Practice it with at least 3 friends or family members.

COVER LETTERS

Cover letters are used for several reasons. One is to introduce you to a contact or a company. It should be concise and action-oriented. The other reason cover letters are used is to respond to an ad on a job board or in the newspaper.

The goal of the cover letter is to demonstrate why you and your background are a good match for the job in question. It should highlight one or two of your unique accomplishments and why you stand out from the crowd. It should not be a lengthy summary of your background.

The cover letter should be a half page in length and follows the following format:

First paragraph:
Introduce yourself and state why you are writing: you are enthusiastically presenting yourself for a specific job and your background makes you the best candidate. List a referral source if possible.

Second paragraph:
List your potential value to the company. Describe how you will contribute and highlight one or two value-added impacts you have made which support the job.

Third paragraph:
State why you're interested in the job, the company, and the industry. Show knowledge of company goals, accomplishments, and opportunities.

Fourth paragraph is a call to action. Ask for the interview and state when you will follow up. Thank them for their time and consideration.

EXAMPLE OF A STANDARD COVER LETTER

June 12, 2008

Ms. Laurie Smith
Human Resources Director
Turbine Entertainment Software
60 Main Street
Medford, MA 02556

Dear Ms. Smith:

I was extremely excited to learn about the Quality Assurance position at Turbine Entertainment Software from Jim Johnson. I'm confident that my passion and knowledge of the gaming industry, as well as my creativity, will make me a strong asset to your organization.

My retail experience at XXX Company enabled me to develop strong customer service skills and to consistently exceed customer expectations.

I am especially excited about the potential opportunity to apply my analytical skills and industry knowledge to the Quality Assurance department at Turbine.

I would appreciate the opportunity to meet with you to see how I can contribute to Turbine. I will call you on Thursday, June 19. In the interim, you can reach me at 414-999-5555. Thank you for your consideration.

Yours sincerely,

John Jones

EXAMPLE OF A COLUMN COVER LETTER

When you are responding to a newspaper ad, we recommend you use a **Column Letter.** This format will quickly highlight your background and how it meets the needs of the job posted. Here is a sample cover letter using the Column Letter approach.

February 2, 2009
Mr. Jake A. Smith
456 Main Street
Chicago, IL 60617

Ms. Susan Jones
Human Resources Manager, ABC Financial
123 Central Street
Chicago, IL 60617

Dear Ms. Jones:

I am writing in response to the Financial Accountant position advertised in the Chicago Sun Times on Sunday, February 2. As you can see, my qualifications closely match your requirements.

Your Requirements	My Qualifications
• 1-2 years accounting experience	• Tracked expenses and prepared all financial reports for fraternity for 2 years
• Attention to detail	• Coordinated a Fun Run for a local charity for 100 runners
• College degree in accounting	• BA in Accounting from ABC University

I would like the opportunity to be considered for this position. Attached please find a copy of my resume. I will plan to call you on Monday, February 10.

Thank you for your time and consideration.

Sincerely,

Jake A. Smith

YOUR COVER LETTER

Now write a cover letter expressing interest in your first choice job title.

REFERENCES

References are another tool you will need. All employers check them, so you will need to decide who would be your best choice. Your best sources of references are professional contacts or people who have experience with you in a work setting, extracurricular activities, college professors, or personal acquaintances.

References

1. Choose three people to provide references for you.
2. Tell them what types of jobs you're interviewing for and why you think you are a good fit and why they would be a good reference.
3. Call them to ask if they are willing to provide a reference.
4. Compile your list of references below. Include their name, title, affiliation with you, and contact information.

REFERENCE NAME	AFFILIATION	CONTACT INFORMATION

THANK YOU NOTES

After every meeting, phone call, or contact given to you, you **must write a thank-you note.** This includes networking, phone calls, and any time someone helps you in your job search.

Thank-you notes are a great way to stay on someone's "radar" for potential future openings. In a job interview situation, thank you notes are the last opportunity you have to sell yourself and reiterate your interest in the job.

Types of Thank-You Notes

Networking/General Contacts:
- Send via e-mail
- Keep it simple
- Opportunity to stay on their radar screen

Job/Informational Interviews:
- Send via hard copy and email
- Opportunity to highlight why you're a good fit for their organization.
- Shows your interest in their organization

DON'T FORGET TO...

✔ Spell the person's name and title correctly!
✔ Use the correct address.
✔ Your note should be professional and show that you were listening during the interview – include a comment about your discussion.
✔ Write a customized note to every person you meet.
✔ Send it via email and follow-up with hard copy.
✔ Be timely – your thank-you note should be sent within 24 hours at the most.
✔ Send a hard copy thank-you note to the hiring manager.

THANK YOU NOTE SAMPLES

Networking Thank-You Note Sample (send via email)

> Dear John,
>
> I wanted to thank you for referring me to Mary Smith at ABC Corporation. I will call Mary this week and will keep you posted on my progress.
>
> Thanks again.
>
> Sally Jones

Job Interview Thank-You Note Sample (send via email within 24 hours and follow-up with a hard copy letter)

> Dear John,
>
> *(purpose of the letter)*
> I wanted to thank you for your time on (Day). I appreciate the opportunity to learn more about ABC Company, in particular the way in which you have structured your sales system.
>
> *(tie your unique qualities to their needs/why they should hire you)*
> As we discussed, I had the opportunity to work on the sales system at XYZ Company and identify where there was misplaced data. Once I communicated the system's needs to the technology group, we were able to execute targeted mailings to the brokers and the sales group was able to follow up with the right people.
>
> *(the close – reiterate your interest and state specific follow-up plans)*
> I am very interested in the Marketing Coordinator position we discussed. I will plan to call you next Monday to determine the next step.
>
> Thank you.
>
> Jane Smith

When you are sending the hard copy follow-up letter, use the standard business letter format from page 91.

MANAGING YOUR NETWORK

Appropriate Follow-up

Once you make that initial contact, each one gets easier. Next, you need to follow up. Follow-up means staying in touch with your contacts so they remember you and keep you in mind when they hear of a job. Follow-up is a critical step in the job search process. Getting people to remember you, especially when they hear of a job lead, is what will get you a job. But, there is a right way to follow up and a wrong way to follow up. You want to be perceived as assertive and enthusiastic, rather than aggressive or demanding. When following up with your contacts, keep these DO's and DON'Ts in mind:

DOs:

- Have a reason to follow up: "I just wanted to follow up to let you know that I am still interested."

- Respect the fact that people are genuinely busy.

- Ask if it's okay to check back in periodically and if email or the phone works better.

- Be polite and professional.

DON'Ts:

- Expect the person to have an answer right away.

- Make more work for them; Instead: "there's no need to call back if nothing has changed."

- Hound the person 3 times per week.

- Demand a response or a job.

Always thank your contact promptly. It can be as simple as sending an email to thank them for the contact/information/interview, although, for a job interview, we recommend sending an email and a follow-up letter via hard copy. (See page 95 for thank-you note tips.) "Promptly" means within **24 hours** of the event. In addition, thank your initial contacts and keep them in the loop on your progress.

TRACKING YOUR PROGRESS

As your job search progresses, you will be surprised how quickly your network will grow. Opportunities you will find from job ads and job boards will grow as well. It's important to track your progress daily—follow-up and persistence are critical to a successful job search, but you will also be creating your own professional network that, if managed well, will serve you for your entire career. Tracking your progress to ensure timely and appropriate follow-up is critical.

Job Search Action Plan

Create your Job Search Action Plan (page 104). The plan will include your daily schedule, which will help you track your progress.

Contact Sheets

Use these for **every** contact you make (see page 99). Once you start making a lot of contacts, it will be very difficult to remember each call. Fill out your sheet as completely as you can, before, during and after the call. Remember to include any pertinent details about the call and the follow-up necessary. For example, if your contact appears to be extremely busy, note that information on the Networking Contact Sheet. Next time you contact that person, be as succinct as possible. ***Networking and Interviewing Contact sheets are located in the back of the book as tear-outs.***

Filing System

Create a filing system that works for you. For some people, filing the contact sheets in a three-ring binder works best; for others, an online tool such as Microsoft Outlook Contact Manager is preferred.

Even an accordion file is a great way to manage your Network/Interview Contact Sheets. Get a file which has numbers from 1-31. When you're networking with someone and they ask you to contact them on the 21st of the month, file their Network Sheet on the 21st. Each morning, when you get up, go into your accordion file to see who you need to contact that day.

Whatever system you choose, it should record all pertinent information and create a tickler file so you can follow up in an appropriate and timely manner.

✏ - NETWORKING CONTACT INFORMATION SHEET

Date: _____

Name: _____   Phone: _____
Company Industry: _____   Address: _____
Job: _____   Address: _____
Email: _____   Referred by: _____

GOAL OF CALL

MY STORY - BULLET POINTS

OPENING STATEMENT

QUESTIONS I WILL ASK	ANSWERS/NOTES

CLOSING: ASK TO FOLLOW-UP OR SET UP INTERVIEW

FOLLOW-UP AND NEXT STEPS

Copy of this page located in Forms section for photocopying if necessary.

INTERVIEW INFORMATION SHEET

Name: _____ Company Industry: _____ Date: _____

GOAL OF CALL

MY STORY - BULLET POINTS

OPENING STATEMENT

QUESTIONS I WILL ASK

ANSWERS/NOTES

CLOSING: ASK TO FOLLOW-UP OR SET UP INTERVIEW

FOLLOW -UP AND NEXT STEPS

Copy of this page located in Forms section for photocopying if necessary.

JOB SEARCH ACTION PLAN

A successful job search requires a plan of action. An effective **Job Search Action Plan** will pull together your goals, background, and the job search strategies that are appropriate for you. It will also help you track your progress.

Below is a sample of an effective **Job Search Action Plan**. Take a few minutes to read through it. Create your own plan before you begin your actual search.

JOB SEARCH ACTION PLAN SAMPLE FOR "ANGELA COOPER"	
Career Goals: My short-term goal is to obtain an entry-level position in the insurance or financial services industry with growth potential, located in the Boston area. My long-term goal is to join an organization which will help me develop my professional skills, learn and grow, gain experience and prepare to attend graduate school.	*Go to page 37 to find your career goals.*
Job Search Strategies: I will use the following strategies in my job search: (Check as many boxes as needed) ❏ Networking (61% success rate) ❏ LinkedIn/Twitter ❏ Career Services from my college ❏ Alumni Services and Associations ❏ Job Boards (Monstertrak.com and Craigslist.com) ❏ Internet searches on companies (research their homepages) ❏ Newspaper ❏ Temporary Agencies ❏ Internships	*Choose what works for your plan.*
Tools to support the plan: Networking Contact List page 85 Your First Call page 87 My Commercial revised page 89 Cover letter template page 93 Resume page 53 Thank-You Note template page 96 Network Contact Sheets page 99 My Story page 46 My Examples page 61 Interview Question Answers page 64-66 Questions for the Interviewer page 67	*This is work you've already done.* *Just pull it together.*

JOB SEARCH ACTION PLAN SAMPLE FOR "ANGELA COOPER"		
Target employer/industry: John Hancock (Manu Life)		*Targeted employers can be found in your Career Goals – page 37 (make copies of this page for additional companies as needed)*
ACTIVITIES	**ACTIONS**	**DONE**
• Networking • Informational interviews • Internships, volunteering, part-time work	❏ Research John Hancock (Manu Life) on the internet ❏ Ask Uncle John if I can talk to his neighbor who works there ❏ Go to Career Services and see if there are any alumnae contacts at John Hancock (Manu Life) or internships	

JOB SEARCH ACTION PLAN SAMPLE FOR "ANGELA COOPER"		
Target employer/industry: Sun Life Insurance Company		*Targeted employers can be found in your Career Goals – page 37.*
ACTIVITIES	**ACTIONS**	**DONE**
• Networking • Informational interviews • Internships, volunteering, part-time work	❏ Research Sun Life ❏ Ask Dad's insurance agent if he has any contacts at Sun Life ❏ Call business professors from school for suggestions on how to approach Sun Life ❏ Call all contacts to set up informational interviews ❏ Apply for a temporary job at Sun Life	

JOB SEARCH ACTION PLAN SAMPLE FOR "ANGELA COOPER"		
Target employer/industry: Mass Financial Services		*Targeted employers can be found in your Career Goals – page 37.*
ACTIVITIES	**ACTIONS**	**DONE**
• Networking	❏ Research Mass Financial Services to find the names of managers for departments such as Customer Service and Sales ❏ Find the name of the Recruiter for these departments	
• Informational interviews	❏ Call the people I've found	
• Internships, volunteering, part-time work	❏ Investigate part-time opportunities	

JOB SEARCH ACTION PLAN SAMPLE FOR "ANGELA COOPER": RECOMMENDED DAILY SCHEDULE	
7:15 a.m.	❏ Prepare your calls for the day ❏ Review your networking list for those who need to be contacted for the first time ❏ Review accordion file for those who need follow up ❏ Prepare each call on your Network Contact Sheets ❏ Do not leave a voice mail until you have tried calling three times
7:45 a.m.	❏ Make the calls ❏ Smile! Show enthusiasm! ❏ Record results on your Network Contact Sheets
8:30 - 11:45 a.m.	❏ Follow-up with contacts ❏ Write thank-you notes ❏ File Network Contact Sheets for follow up ❏ Research, interviews, meetings
11:45 a.m.	❏ Call-backs from this morning
12:30 p.m.	❏ Follow up from morning calls
5:00 p.m.	❏ Call-backs. Remember the 3 call rule - if this is your 3rd try leave a message
5:30 p.m.	❏ Same day follow-up from your calls ❏ Send thank-you notes; email and hard copy for the first time calls; email only for a repeat call ❏ Send out resumes when appropriate
This schedule can vary from person to person. *Set a schedule that works best for you and "just do it".*	

➤ Now it's time for you to complete your **Job Search Action Plan**.

CAREER GOALS

JOB SEARCH STRATEGIES

I will use the following strategies in my job search: (Check as many boxes as needed)

❑ Networking (61% success rate)
❑ LinkedIn/Twitter
❑ Career Services from my college
❑ Alumni Services and Associations
❑ Job Boards (Monstertrak.com and Craigslist.com)
❑ Internet searches on companies (research their homepages)
❑ Newspaper
❑ Temporary Agencies
❑ Internships

TOOLS TO HELP SUPPORT YOUR PLAN

Networking Contact List	page 85
Your First Call	page 87
My Commercial revised	page 89
Cover letter template	page 93
Resume	page 53
Thank You Note template	page 96
Network Contact Sheets	page 99
My Story	page 46
My Examples	page 61
Interview Question Answers	page 64-66
Questions for the Interviewer	page 67

Copy of this page located in Forms section for photocopying if necessary.

Targeted employers/industries

EMPLOYER: _____

ACTIVITIES	ACTIONS	DONE
Networking		
Informational interviews		
Internships, volunteering, part-time work		

EMPLOYER: _____

ACTIVITIES	ACTIONS	DONE
Networking		
Informational interviews		
Internships, volunteering, part-time work		

Copy of this page located in Forms section for photocopying if necessary.

YOUR DAILY SCHEDULE		
DAY/WEEK OF	**ACTIVITY**	**RESULTS/NEXT STEP**
MONDAY	❑ ❑ ❑ ❑ ❑ ❑	
TUESDAY	❑ ❑ ❑ ❑ ❑ ❑	
WEDNESDAY	❑ ❑ ❑ ❑ ❑ ❑	
THURSDAY	❑ ❑ ❑ ❑ ❑ ❑	
FRIDAY	❑ ❑ ❑ ❑ ❑ ❑	

Copy of this page located in Forms section for photocopying if necessary.

TIPS FOR COMPLETING A JOB APPLICATION

Most organizations will require that you complete a job application at some point in the interview process. Here are some tips:

☑ Print your answers, as opposed to cursive writing. Use a pen and your best handwriting. Neatness counts.

☑ Try to answer every question. If a question doesn't apply to you, just write "not applicable".

☑ Do not give an expected salary. Simply write "negotiable" if there is a salary question.

☑ Make sure all names are spelled correctly and phone numbers are clear and legible.

☑ Be honest about everything: why you left a job, your education, or any employment gaps. Most organizations perform security checks on all candidates, and if you are not honest, you will not be hired.

☑ Remember to bring the phone numbers of your references with you.

☑ Don't forget to sign and date the application.

HANDLING REJECTION

When you don't get the job...

You've done all the right things (or so you thought), but you didn't get the job. All may not be lost. We recommend that you call your contact back the next day and ask them why you didn't get the job. Remember to be polite and respect the fact that they made their decision. You might say:

> "I want to let you know that I am so interested in that position and I thought it would be a good match. Can you give me some feedback so I will know more in the future?"

Contacting the company after a rejection and asking for feedback gives you an opportunity to clarify anything in your background which may be of interest to them in the future. It's possible that you were their second choice or the position was cut. If that's the case, ask if it's okay to periodically email or call back regarding any future openings. If there was something about you that they didn't like, listen to what they have to say and act on it the next time. This can be a great opportunity to learn more about yourself or to have another chance at getting the job.

Determine what you learned from this situation and move on.

Make the next call!

SALARY NEGOTIATIONS

You got the offer! It's the right job and company for you. Now what? Thank the recruiter (or manager) for the offer. The recruiter will probably make the offer verbally, including your salary and benefits. They should then send it to you in writing. It is always a good idea to ask if you can have some time to think it over. Ask how long you have to make a decision.

Make sure you understand the offer, including the title, responsibilities, the manager and the compensation. Remember that there is more than one component to compensation: there is a base salary, but there may also be the potential for a bonus or other cash compensation. The benefits package can also significantly add $$ to your offer. Ask them to explain the components of the compensation.

If you are unhappy with the offer you received, here are a few tips to negotiating your compensation package.

- Know ahead of time what the job pays. Research the type of job on a compensation website such as www.salary.com or by looking it up in the Occupational Outlook Handbook, www.bls.gov/oco

- Understand your priorities. How much do you need to pay your bills? What is the absolute minimum you can accept? Keep in mind that career growth opportunities can be more important in the long run than extra cash in the short run.

- When speaking to the recruiter, be professional and polite. Remember, you both want the same thing. Offers have been known to be rescinded because the salary negotiations became antagonistic.

- Understand that, although many things are negotiable, some things are not. For example, if you are joining a large corporate training program with other recruits, there may not be any negotiation in the salary for fear of discrimination.

- Ask about benefits - many companies can send you a brochure about what they can offer. Take the time to read through it and ask for clarification on those items you don't understand.

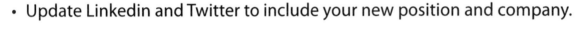

ENDING YOUR JOB SEARCH

Congratulations, you accepted the job offer. You're getting ready for your first day. You think you're finished, right?

Wrong! There are a few things you need to do before you close this chapter.

- First, you need to inform your network. This means letting everyone who helped you know of your success. Be sure to let them know what you'll be doing and where. Thank your contacts for their help and let them know that you're happy to help them in any way you can in the future. This can be done by brief, individual (not mass) emails.

- Next, be sure to organize all of your contact and interview sheets. Create a plan for keeping in touch with your network so that you're always managing your career.

- You may consider calling your new boss to ask if there is anything you can do or read before your start date. This will go a long way in making a good first impression.

- Update Linkedin and Twitter to include your new position and company.

SUCCEED

"When you are starting your career, your goals should be to build a strong work record."
— *Business Week* Magazine

Getting Ready For the First Day: It's here...your first day on the new job. It can be exciting and anxiety producing. Here are some tips to help make it more successful. You've made a great first impression on the people who hired you. Now it's time to make a great first impression on everyone else.

Make sure you:

- Complete any pre-employment paperwork given to you. Complete it carefully and on time. Bring your license, passport, or picture ID with you on the first day. You will need this for identification.
- Know what your company does and how your role contributes to it.
- Make sure you know your exact title and manager's name.
- Choose your outfit the night before. Dress conservatively!
- Have a good breakfast on your first day.
- Arrive at work at exactly the time you were given. You will have plenty of opportunities to come in early and stay late (to impress people) as time goes on.
- Bring a portfolio with paper and two pens with you on the first day. You will need them!
- Make sure you understand all the paperwork you are asked to complete, especially tax forms and employee benefit forms.
- Learn co-workers' names and what they do. Write them down if you need to. Everyone likes to be called by name.
- Don't bring anything to personalize your work space at first. Wait and see what your co-workers have done and then you can follow suit.
- Understand that you will be exhausted after your first few days...starting a new job is hard work!

Creating a Daily Routine to Succeed:

- Become a morning person and always arrive (at minimum) on time.
- Be the first person in the office to say hello in the morning. Say it with a smile.
- Plan your day in advance. Some people like to use a "to-do" list, some people use an online calendar. Use whatever works best for you. Be sure to list all your tasks in order of priority.
- Arrive at meetings on time. Bring extra work or business-related reading that you can do while you wait for the others.
- Periodically check your appearance throughout the day.
- Try to stay late whenever you can.

THE KEYS TO SUCCESS

Having been in school for 16+ years, you learned how to succeed in an academic setting. You learned how to argue what you thought about a book or an assignment with passion. You learned that, in school, you get frequent and concrete feedback, and you learned the importance of developing independent thoughts and ideas. Unfortunately, some of those very skills that you have mastered in school can get you into trouble in the world of work.

Do the things you like to do least first thing in the morning! You will be surprised at how much more you accomplish throughout the day!

The transition from the world of education to the world of work is probably one of the biggest you will ever make. The good news is that there are some very specific things you can do to shine during this transition. So few people take the time to plan their transition, it makes it easy for you to look good. We call these "things" our Keys to Success.

🔑 Keys to Success

1. Adopt the Right Attitude.
- Show a positive attitude and a strong work ethic.
- Everyone thinks they work hard, but they don't.
- Be early for work and stay late to help out. • Volunteer for extra projects.
- All of this will help make you stand out. • Be flexible.
- Life in the world of work is full of changes, and they are not always fair.
- Your colleagues know you are smart. Now show them you can learn.

Treat secretaries & other assistants with respect! They can make or break you!

2. Adjust Your Expectations.
- Most first jobs are not as glamorous or as challenging as we dream them to be.
- Do the small (a.k.a., menial) tasks first and do them well. It builds trust. The "good" stuff will come later.

3. Earn Respect from Your Co-workers.
- Understand that you are new to an organization and you need to build a good reputation for yourself.
- Quietly get the job done to the best of your ability.
- Build a track record: become known as dependable and willing to work hard at whatever the task is.
- A strong track record will protect you when inevitable mistakes happen.

Don't tell or listen to sexist or racist jokes. It's unprofessional and in some cases, illegal.

4. Build Effective Relationships.

Building effective relationships is just as important
(and sometimes more important) as doing the job.
Much of what you will need to know isn't written down;
you will have to get that information from your co-workers.

College is
a great place for
complaining.
The working
world is
the place
for doing!!

- Say good morning to people; listen to others.
- Understand that work relationships are different from your relationships
  with your friends. Your co-workers may be older and in a different lifestyle. Try to find things
  that you have in common.
- Learn to work in teams: Be sure to credit the whole team when given compliments
  about the work completed.

5. Be An Easy Employee To Manage...every boss appreciates it!

Your relationship with your boss is critical. The reality is that managing people is very difficult,
and few managers do it well. As a result, you have to make it work.

- Talk to your co-workers to find out how much information your boss likes to receive.
  Does he/she like regular updates, or do they only want to hear about problems?
- What can you do to make your boss look good?
- Understand your boss not only has to manage you and your co-workers, but also his/her
  boss. You can't get all of his/her attention.

6. Use Appropriate Communications Skills.

- Find out how people communicate.
- Do they use text, email, IM, voicemail?
- How is email used?
- Your emails should be grammatically correct with dictionary spelling
  and proper punctuation.
- Is email used to disseminate information only, or is it used instead
  of a face-to- face meeting?
- Be careful how you compose your emails. Intentions can be misconstrued.
- Be conscious of the format used for business writing within
  your company. Some organizations prefer a bulleted format;
  some prefer long-hand with detailed paragraphs.
- Voice mail etiquette - keep it short, always leave your phone
  number or extension. If possible, listen to the message you are
  leaving before you send it to make sure you sound concise and
  professional.

Don't tell your
boss you have
nothing to do!
Go to them with
a suggestion!
Works like
a charm!

Mistakes on the job
happen – own up to
them immediately.
Apologize and
figure out why. Seek
additional training
if needed!

BEWARE: TECHNOLOGY IN THE WORKPLACE

Most companies provide the technology you will need to get the job done. Keep in mind that these tools should be used for business reasons only. Managers can and do track websites visited, emails sent and received, and instant messaging.

A word about emails...they live forever

• no jokes

• no sensitive information

• no angry or arrogant tones

• no pictures

UNDERSTAND YOUR COMPANY'S CULTURE AND ADAPT TO IT

A company's culture is how it operates. Every organization has a unique culture, and it shapes everything from how you work to what you wear.

What is the "culture"?

• Is it an ever-changing environment, or a static environment?

• Are you expected to work independently, or are there policies which govern how you get your work done?

• What gets rewarded? Is it face time (the number of hours you put in), or do they manage for results?

• Is the required dress professional, or is it business-casual?

You can learn about the culture by watching those around you and asking others for help. You are already in the process of building good relationships, so asking people won't be a problem.

DEVELOP WORK SMARTS

Skills such as time management, juggling projects, business writing, and public speaking will help you become an outstanding performer. Take the time and initiative to continue to develop and improve these skills.

Keys to Success:

DOs	DON'Ts
Display a positive attitude and work ethic.	Gossip or complain.
Adjust your expectations.	Try to change your job on the first day.
Earn respect from your co-workers.	Be a "know it all".
Build effective relationships.	Be too needy—be resourceful instead.
Become an employee who is easy to manage.	Isolate yourself—build good work relationships and keep in touch with your friends and contacts. It helps to keep a good balance.
Understand the culture and adapt to it.	
Develop work smarts.	Use workplace computers and other technology for personal reasons.
Use technology appropriately.	

HOW TO HANDLE DISAPPOINTMENT ON THE JOB

You've worked hard...you worked hard to get into college and you worked hard to get out of college. You worked hard to establish your career goals, and you worked hard to get the job you wanted.

Now, your boss has just asked you to make 30 copies of a presentation he's giving at 1:00. Next, your co-worker asked you to cover the phones so he can go to the dentist. Finally, the project you wanted and lobbied for was given to someone else. Is this what you went to college for? What do you do?

1. Take deep breaths and count slowly to 10.

2. Smile and complete the task at hand to the best of your ability.

3. Remember your career goals. Keep your long-term goals in mind to avoid resentment (and yes, people can tell you are resentful and may even expect it from a young professional). You are always learning and getting experience no matter what the task. Connect what you are doing now with what you want to do in the long term. Revisiting your career goals periodically will help you to stay on track in the short term.

DEVELOP YOUR CAREER

Now that you've started on your career path, take this opportunity to enjoy the work you're doing and learn everything you can. This is the time to continue building your skills and increase your responsibilities. It is also the time to develop yourself professionally. Some ways you can do this are:

• Participate in company-sponsored training programs.

• Become aware of what's going on in your industry by reading trade journals and company newsletters.

• Ask questions—be inquisitive.

• You can also take a night course to build your general business skills and knowledge.

You own your career. Take advantage of all of the opportunities around you.

SELF-ASSESSMENT - THINGS TO THINK ABOUT ON THE JOB

Here are some questions you should ask yourself when you start your job, and then reassess your answers periodically.

QUESTION	ANSWER	HOW AM I DOING?
What kind of employee do I want to be?		
Who do I need to please and impress? What will it take to make a good impression?		
How can I make them think I respect and admire them?		
How do I support and win-over my co-workers?		
Who seems to be the most difficult to work with? How will I handle that?		
How will I develop my internal network of supporters?		
What are my competitive advantages that can boost my status? How can I use them without alienating others?		
Who is my "best" friend at work? Who can I trust to tell me how I am doing politically?		

Identifying and finding the right job is a life skill that will help you manage your career in any type of job market environment.

Assessing your skills, interests, and workplace needs is an often-overlooked step, but you now know that it is the driver in any successful job search. Presenting yourself articulately and with confidence is the first step in creating a positive impression. Using creativity and face-to-face networking when conducting your actual job search significantly increases your chances of success.

The skills you mastered in this book can and should be used throughout your career when your job needs take you in a different direction.

If you are interested in working with a Career Coach or have questions, please visit us on-line at CareerTreking.com. You will find job search tips as well as updated job information to help you manage your career.

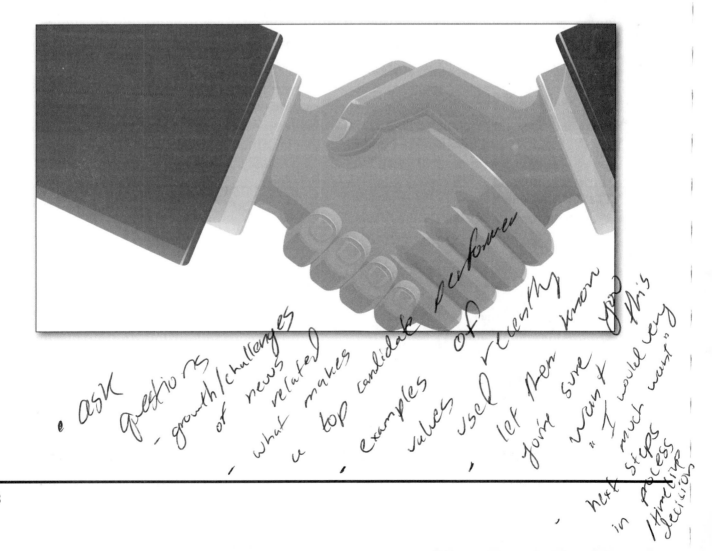

Notes with Lori

- long term career goals
  , its leadership development
  for your career
- how committed are you?
- building your career,
  international mobility
  (moving around & developing
  career

- think through **FORMS** job description

memorable give strong examples through
details→ storytelling (STAR formula)
- data dump
- talk about team work,
  be humble but make
  they <u>know</u> what you've done
  , when did you take
  leadership
- time experiences & interests to
  CAT values
- show you've done additional
  research
(annual reports, press releases)

119

INFORMATIONAL INTERVIEW EVALUATION WORKSHEET

This worksheet should be used in the informational interview process to help you evaluate potential career opportunities. Use it to write down your thoughts, questions and observations following the interview.

Career/Job Title: _____ Interviewee: _____ Date: _____

CATEGORY	OBSERVATION
What did you like the most about this industry, job or career track? *(What seemed challenging, rewarding or satisfying to you?)*	
What did you dislike?	
What did you learn about the daily tasks and responsibilities?	
What are the skills and experience required for this position/career? Are there training/career path opportunities?	
Are there gaps between your background and the job/career requirements?	
Who else should you talk to about this or related job fields?	

Are you interested in this career opportunity/industry/job?   Yes   No

(Circle one)

INDUSTRY ANALYSIS

Listed below are some questions to help you in your research of various industries. Record your answers in the chart below.

Industry _____

QUESTIONS TO ASK	ANSWERS
What product or service does this industry offer?	
What determines success in this industry?	
Is this industry hiring?	
What type of talent does this industry need?	
Do I have some of these skills from past work experience or internships?	
Does the subject matter of this industry relate to my favorite subjects in school or areas of interest?	
What is the work environment like? Does it line up with my work values?	

JOB ANALYSIS:

JOB TITLE/CAREER	SKILLS AND EXPERIENCE REQUIRED	SKILLS AND EXPERIENCE I HAVE	GAP

KEY TASKS AND RESPONSIBILITIES	WORK ENVIRONMENT	CAREER & FINANCIAL OPPORTUNITIES	LIFESTYLE/LOCATION

List companies and 3 reasons why you want to work for them here.

COMPANY NAME	REASON 1	REASON 2	REASON 3

Questions to Think About

What are the Company's key products & services?

How is this Company different from others in industry?

What are the Company's values and culture?

How are employees treated?

Are there opportunities for good experience, training, & growth?

CONTACT TRACKING LIST

MY CONTACTS	HOW I KNOW THEM	WHERE THEY WORK

CONTACT TRACKING LIST

MY CONTACTS	HOW I KNOW THEM	WHERE THEY WORK

CAREER GOALS

JOB SEARCH STRATEGIES

I will use the following strategies in my job search: (Check as many boxes as needed)

❏ Networking (61% success rate)
❏ LinkedIn/Twitter
❏ Career Services from my college
❏ Alumni Services and Associations
❏ Job Boards (Monstertrak.com and Craigslist.com)
❏ Internet searches on companies (research their homepages)
❏ Newspaper
❏ Temporary Agencies
❏ Internships

TOOLS TO HELP SUPPORT YOUR PLAN

Networking Contact List	page 85
Your First Call	page 87
My Commercial revised	page 89
Cover letter template	page 93
Resume	page 53
Thank You Note template	page 96
Network Contact Sheets	page 99
My Story	page 46
My Examples	page 61
Interview Question Answers	page 64-66
Questions for the Interviewer	page 67

Targeted employers/industries

EMPLOYER: _____

ACTIVITIES	ACTIONS	DONE
Networking		
Informational interviews		
Internships, volunteering, part time work		

EMPLOYER: _____

ACTIVITIES	ACTIONS	DONE
Networking		
Informational interviews		
Internships, volunteering, part time work		

YOUR DAILY SCHEDULE		
DAY/WEEK OF	**ACTIVITY**	**RESULTS/NEXT STEP**
MONDAY	❏ ❏ ❏ ❏ ❏ ❏	
TUESDAY	❏ ❏ ❏ ❏ ❏ ❏	
WEDNESDAY	❏ ❏ ❏ ❏ ❏ ❏	
THURSDAY	❏ ❏ ❏ ❏ ❏ ❏	
FRIDAY	❏ ❏ ❏ ❏ ❏ ❏	

YOUR DAILY SCHEDULE		
DAY/WEEK OF	**ACTIVITY**	**RESULTS/NEXT STEP**
MONDAY	❑ ❑ ❑ ❑ ❑ ❑	
TUESDAY	❑ ❑ ❑ ❑ ❑ ❑	
WEDNESDAY	❑ ❑ ❑ ❑ ❑ ❑	
THURSDAY	❑ ❑ ❑ ❑ ❑ ❑	
FRIDAY	❑ ❑ ❑ ❑ ❑ ❑	

NETWORKING CONTACT INFORMATION SHEET

Date: _____

Name: _____   Phone: _____
Company Industry: _____   Address: _____
Job: _____   Address: _____
Email: _____   Referred by: _____

GOAL OF CALL

MY STORY - BULLET POINTS

OPENING STATEMENT

QUESTIONS I WILL ASK	ANSWERS/NOTES

CLOSING: ASK TO FOLLOW-UP OR SET UP INTERVIEW

FOLLOW -UP AND NEXT STEPS

INTERVIEW INFORMATION SHEET

Name: _____ Company Industry: _____ Date: _____

GOAL OF CALL

MY STORY - BULLET POINTS

OPENING STATEMENT

QUESTIONS I WILL ASK	ANSWERS/NOTES

CLOSING: ASK TO FOLLOW-UP OR SET UP INTERVIEW

FOLLOW UP AND NEXT STEPS

NETWORKING CONTACT INFORMATION SHEET

Date: _____

Name: _____   Phone: _____
Company Industry: _____   Address: _____
Job: _____   Address: _____
Email: _____   Referred by: _____

GOAL OF CALL

MY STORY - BULLET POINTS

OPENING STATEMENT

QUESTIONS I WILL ASK	ANSWERS/NOTES

CLOSING: ASK TO FOLLOW-UP OR SET UP INTERVIEW

FOLLOW -UP AND NEXT STEPS

INTERVIEW INFORMATION SHEET

Name: _____ Company Industry: _____ Date: _____

GOAL OF CALL

MY STORY - BULLET POINTS

OPENING STATEMENT

QUESTIONS I WILL ASK	ANSWERS/NOTES

CLOSING: ASK TO FOLLOW-UP OR SET UP INTERVIEW

FOLLOW UP AND NEXT STEPS

NETWORKING CONTACT INFORMATION SHEET

Date: _____

Name: _____   Phone: _____
Company Industry: _____   Address: _____
Job: _____   Address: _____
Email: _____   Referred by: _____

GOAL OF CALL

MY STORY - BULLET POINTS

OPENING STATEMENT

QUESTIONS I WILL ASK	ANSWERS/NOTES

CLOSING: ASK TO FOLLOW-UP OR SET UP INTERVIEW

FOLLOW -UP AND NEXT STEPS

INTERVIEW INFORMATION SHEET

Name: _____ Company Industry: _____ Date: _____

GOAL OF CALL

MY STORY - BULLET POINTS

OPENING STATEMENT

QUESTIONS I WILL ASK

ANSWERS/NOTES

CLOSING: ASK TO FOLLOW-UP OR SET UP INTERVIEW

FOLLOW UP AND NEXT STEPS

NETWORKING CONTACT INFORMATION SHEET

Date: _____

Name: _____ Phone: _____

Company Industry: _____ Address: _____

Job: _____ Address: _____

Email: _____ Referred by: _____

GOAL OF CALL

MY STORY - BULLET POINTS

OPENING STATEMENT

QUESTIONS I WILL ASK

ANSWERS/NOTES

CLOSING: ASK TO FOLLOW-UP OR SET UP INTERVIEW

FOLLOW -UP AND NEXT STEPS

INTERVIEW INFORMATION SHEET

Name: _____ Company Industry: _____ Date: _____

GOAL OF CALL

MY STORY - BULLET POINTS

OPENING STATEMENT

QUESTIONS I WILL ASK	ANSWERS/NOTES

CLOSING: ASK TO FOLLOW-UP OR SET UP INTERVIEW

FOLLOW UP AND NEXT STEPS

NETWORKING CONTACT INFORMATION SHEET

Date: _____

Name: _____ Phone: _____
Company Industry: _____ Address: _____
Job: _____ Address: _____
Email: _____ Referred by: _____

GOAL OF CALL

MY STORY - BULLET POINTS

OPENING STATEMENT

QUESTIONS I WILL ASK	ANSWERS/NOTES

CLOSING: ASK TO FOLLOW-UP OR SET UP INTERVIEW

FOLLOW -UP AND NEXT STEPS

INTERVIEW INFORMATION SHEET

Name: _____ Company Industry: _____ Date: _____

GOAL OF CALL

MY STORY - BULLET POINTS

OPENING STATEMENT

QUESTIONS I WILL ASK	ANSWERS/NOTES

CLOSING: ASK TO FOLLOW-UP OR SET UP INTERVIEW

FOLLOW UP AND NEXT STEPS

NETWORKING CONTACT INFORMATION SHEET

Date: _____

Name: _____   Phone: _____

Company Industry: _____   Address: _____

Job: _____   Address: _____

Email: _____   Referred by: _____

GOAL OF CALL

MY STORY - BULLET POINTS

OPENING STATEMENT

QUESTIONS I WILL ASK	**ANSWERS/NOTES**

CLOSING: ASK TO FOLLOW-UP OR SET UP INTERVIEW

FOLLOW -UP AND NEXT STEPS

INTERVIEW INFORMATION SHEET

Name: _____ Company Industry: _____ Date: _____

GOAL OF CALL

MY STORY - BULLET POINTS

OPENING STATEMENT

QUESTIONS I WILL ASK	ANSWERS/NOTES

CLOSING: ASK TO FOLLOW-UP OR SET UP INTERVIEW

FOLLOW UP AND NEXT STEPS

NETWORKING CONTACT INFORMATION SHEET

Date: _____

Name: _____   Phone: _____

Company Industry: _____   Address: _____

Job: _____   Address: _____

Email: _____   Referred by: _____

GOAL OF CALL

MY STORY - BULLET POINTS

OPENING STATEMENT

QUESTIONS I WILL ASK	ANSWERS/NOTES

CLOSING: ASK TO FOLLOW-UP OR SET UP INTERVIEW

FOLLOW -UP AND NEXT STEPS

INTERVIEW INFORMATION SHEET

Name: _____ Company Industry: _____ Date: _____

GOAL OF CALL

MY STORY - BULLET POINTS

OPENING STATEMENT

QUESTIONS I WILL ASK	ANSWERS/NOTES

CLOSING: ASK TO FOLLOW-UP OR SET UP INTERVIEW

FOLLOW UP AND NEXT STEPS